D1572911

MEDITERRANEAN DIET INSTANT POT COOKBOOK

The Complete Mediterranean Diet Guide with Easy and Delicious
Recipes for Living Better and Life-long Health

Penny Blakoer

CONTENT

Introduction

As a self-proclaimed diet enthusiast, I have always found it challenging to express my passion for food while following a healthy diet plan. Many of the diets available on the internet today will enforce rigid rules and give you a list of forbidden foods. While this is manageable for the first couple of weeks, soon enough the diet becomes too constraining and therefore fails to become a lifestyle. The Mediterranean diet caught me off-guard. I had never been on a diet that mimicked the meals I usually prepare at home. Upon closer examination, I learned that the Mediterranean diet was based on the traditional eating habits in countries bordering the Mediterranean sea. There wasn't necessarily a standard diet plan because the eating styles along the Mediterranean vary. However, there were some common eating traditions that were practiced by these countries, which have inspired others across the world to adopt the Mediterranean way of life.

The intention of this cookbook is to expose you to some of the secrets of Mediterranean cooking that can improve your well-being, lower the risk of diseases, and help you lose weight. Since the diet is more than just a meal plan, I will also teach you how to adopt a Mediterranean lifestyle so that you can live a long and fulfilling life! I will also show you how to prepare Mediterranean-inspired meals in an instant using our beloved kitchen gadget—the Instant Pot. The Instant Pot will take the stress out of preparing healthy meals and allow you to enjoy Michelin star-worthy dishes. You are no longer required to be an expert in the kitchen to serve expert dishes because the Instant Pot will do the work for you! This book will take you on a journey to the Mediterranean and expose you to a healthier way of living.

Chapter 1: The Mediterranean Diet 101

It's More than a Diet, It's a Lifestyle!

Not only is the Mediterranean diet one of the safest and healthiest eating plans for weight-loss, but it is also the most user-friendly due to its flexibility. People can easily modify the diet to suit their lifestyle and still achieve amazing weight-loss results. As a result of how flexible it is, it can soon become a lifestyle instead of a passing diet fad. The Mediterranean diet is rooted in the traditional eating practices of countries along the Mediterranean sea. Their food was mostly plant-based, placing an emphasis on foods like fruit, vegetables, nuts, beans, avocados, olive oil, and seeds. Lean protein was also consumed in moderation and would typically include lean white meat, eggs, cheese, and yogurt. One of the most important things to remember about the Mediterranean diet is that it is a way of living. This means that while there are favored foods, you can still enjoy a glass of wine or a slice of cake every once in a while. It does not require an "all or nothing" approach to preparing meals and therefore anyone can easily maintain it for longer.

A Snapshot of the Mediterranean Diet in a Pyramid

All that the diet requires from you is the commitment to incorporate more healthy foods in your meals and decrease those foods that are less supportive of your health. This does not mean cutting out certain food groups and feeling bad about yourself when you have a slip-up. On the Mediterranean diet, you can indulge in your guilty pleasures occasionally while maintaining a healthy eating lifestyle.

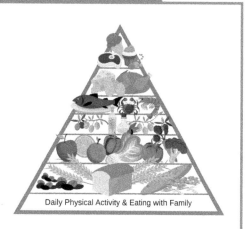

Daily Physical Activity & Eating with Family

So what exactly does the Mediterranean diet look like? We can understand how the diet works by looking at it in terms of a pyramid. The bottom of the pyramid includes those foods that you should eat more of and the top of the pyramid includes the foods that you should consume sparingly. Below is a demonstration of the 7 levels of foods that would be included in a Mediterranean diet, with level 1 being at the bottom of the pyramid:

Level 1: Whole fruits and vegetables, nuts, seeds, beans, and other legumes. Fresh salads that consist of dark leafy lettuce or spinach, fresh tomatoes, cucumbers, broccoli, and onions. Since vegetables will play a significant role in most meals, you can prepare them in various ways such as using them in salads, adding them to appetizers, or as a side dish. Most of the time, fruits are served as a day-time snack or incorporated in desserts. Beans and legumes taste delicious when added to soups, stews, dips such as hummus, or salads.

Level 2: Oats and quinoa, brown rice, millet or millet bread, and sweet potatoes. If you are gluten sensitive or trying to lose weight, avoid consuming standard potatoes, bread, or white pastas. Nonetheless, if you do decide to enjoy these foods, consume them in moderation (serving size of a tennis ball for women and two tennis balls for men).

Level 3: Olive oil is preferred over other oils, butters, and margarines, however, you can use different oils to achieve various flavors in your meals. Oil is not only used for cooking foods. It can also be used in combination with balsamic vinegar to create a salad dressing or drizzled on bread, soups, and other sauces.

Level 4: Dairy products such as cheese and yogurts should be consumed in small amounts. For instance, you can grate some Parmesan cheese on pasta dishes or dice feta cheese on salads. Those who love yogurt should try to limit it to a cup a day and served with some delicious fresh fruits. Yogurt is also a great ingredient to use in curries and salad dressings due to its naturally smooth and creamy flavor. If you are sensitive to dairy, reduce your yogurt intake to about once every four days or find dairy-free yogurts.

Level 5: Fish should be eaten more than other meats because of the vitamins that are loaded in it. For example, you can consume between 4 to 6 ounce-portions of fish several times per week. When it comes to selecting the healthiest option, choose low-mercury fish like anchovies, catfish, crab, haddock, hake, salmon, or whitefish (just to name a few).

Level 6: When eating poultry, stick to lean options such as turkey, duck, chicken, or ostrich. In terms of a serving suggestion, you can consume around 3 to 6 ounce-portions of chicken a few times per week. You can also incorporate eggs in your meals, however, try to keep the serving between 2 to 6 eggs per week. Of course, the egg white is healthier than the yolk and therefore a ratio of 1 yolk to 3 egg whites will offer you better health benefits.

Level 7: Red meat is also allowed on this diet. Meats such as beef, veal, lamb, and goat can be enjoyed in 3 to 6 ounce-portions once or twice a week (or a few times a month). There are many other ways of serving red meat other than making it a side on your plate. For example, you can cut it in thin slices and top it on salads, pastas, or alternatively combine it in rice dishes.

Eating for Health and Well-being

The Mediterranean diet is all about eating for optimum health. Even though it does not restrict people from eating certain foods, there are always foods that provide you with more vitamins and nutritional value than others. For example, whole grains are favored over empty carbs. The reason why whole-grain foods such as brown rice are better than refined grains such as white rice is due to the presence of fiber in these foods. Whole-grain foods consist of bran which offers many essential nutrients to your body. The fiber in whole grains slows down the absorption of sugars into your bloodstream so that you have a more sustained supply of energy throughout the day. Mediterranean diets also favor good fats from bad fats. For example, saturated fats found in meat and dairy products should be consumed in moderation due to the health risks that are associated with these fats. Instead, you can consume more unsaturated fats found in fish, vegetables, and nuts which will improve your heart health and overall well-being.

To experience the full measure of health benefits on this diet, it is recommended that you eat certain foods in moderation. For instance, it is generally not a good idea (whether practicing the Mediterranean diet or not) to consume highly processed foods and beverages such as  frozen meals, candy, and sodas. These foods are usually very high in sodium, sugars, and carbohydrates leading to weight gain and other health-related risks. However, if you are purchasing a packaged food that closely resembles its whole-food form, then it is safe to eat. An example of this would be purchasing canned beans which are processed however, they are still in its whole-food form. It is also recommended that you limit your intake of juices such as fruit or vegetable juices (whether processed or not). Juices contain a lot of sugar and this could lead to you having sugar spikes throughout the day. When you do drink a glass of juice, add water (or drink a glass of water afterward) so that you can dilute the amount of sugar in the drink.

 Alcohol is also permitted on the Mediterranean diet, however, it must be consumed in moderation. When choosing the best alcoholic beverage to drink, opt for red wine which carries a lot of health benefits, particularly for your heart. Women should generally limit their alcohol intake to one glass per day and up to two glasses per day for men. Smoking of any kind will have to be paused or completely halted when practicing the Mediterranean diet. There are no health benefits that can be obtained from smoking, and in most cases, smoking can lead to organ failure and other serious health diseases. There are many resources and forums online to help you quit smoking and adopt healthier habits. One of the more encouraging habits to accompany the Mediterranean diet is incorporating regular exercise in your week to boost your overall health. Beginners can start off by taking a brisk walk twice a week and as you become fitter, you can incorporate other cardio exercises that will strengthen your vital organs.

Chapter 2: Mediterranean Cooking Made Instant

For many of us, adopting the Mediterranean diet is the smart choice. Over the years, there have been numerous studies showing us how this diet can lead to weight loss, improve our brain and heart health, and lower our risk of contracting diseases such as diabetes or high blood pressure. However, changing the way we eat is still not as easy as it looks. Any kind of diet, whether it is restrictive or not, requires us to actually spend time thinking about our food decisions. This means that we cannot mindlessly put ingredients into our trolleys or grab takeaways on a Friday night like we used to. Every food item needs to be considered and assessed on whether it adds value to our diet or not. Those who are cooking for their families will also need to consider ways of accommodating their family's needs while also sticking to the diet plan. All of this decision-making can be exhausting!

Nowadays, we simply don't have the time to think about small decisions like meal preparation when we have other overwhelming demands and pressures in our lives. For many people, spending 45 minutes to an hour cooking late at night or on the weekends is a chore and not a delightful activity. The Instant Pot has become the modern way of cooking because it answers many of our grievances when it comes to cooking healthy and quick meals. It performs the cooking functions that you would traditionally perform at a fraction of the time. While the Instant Pot is preparing your food, you can continue with other tasks and chores around the household. And what's more, the Instant Pot transforms any recipe into a high-quality dish that would be served in restaurants.

The Instant Pot is a great kitchen gadget to use when preparing your Mediterranean diet recipes. It will allow you to steam vegetables, prepare hearty stews, or whip up a delicious soup in minutes. Once you learn how to use the Instant Pot correctly, you can prepare Mediterranean-inspired meals instantly. Your meats will come out tender and your vegetables cooked through to perfection. The Instant Pot will also help you make soups, sauces, and broths that are delicious when served with fresh crusty bread with a drizzle of olive oil.

You Have a Chef in Your Kitchen— Instant Pot

An Instant Pot is a type of electric pressure cooker that works by generating heat under a tight seal so that it can reach higher temperatures than normal stove pots without the steam escaping. The steam from the Instant Pot cooks food a lot quicker than traditional cooking methods such as stovetop or oven cooking. When high heat and pressure is added, meals are prepared much faster without the quality of the ingredients being compromised. The only caveat is that you need to allow the gadget enough time to heat up before you can use it.

Since pressure is required for cooking, the Instant Pot needs around 15 to 20 minutes to preheat and come to pressure before food can be added. Moreover, when preparing dishes like meat, you will need extra time to allow the pressure to release gradually after cooking. When pressure is released right away, it can make your meat come out tough and not as tender as you would like. An extra 10 to 2o minutes of a gradual release of pressure will continue the cooking process until the meat is ready to be served.

The Mechanics of Cooking with an Instant Pot

An Instant Pot provides you with the convenience of preparing a hearty Mediterranean-inspired family meal in less than 30 minutes. You can cook rice, stew vegetables, or roast a full chicken from start to finish and only come back to check on your dish when it is time to serve it up! Who would have thought that one gadget could bake bread, braise meat, or cook dry beans that usually need to be soaked in water overnight, within minutes? The range of functions that an Instant Pot offers is only useful when you know how to program the machine. Depending on the recipe that you are making, you will program your Instant Pot differently, however, many recipes—especially those that involve meat—will follow the simple formula below:

Step 1: Set your Instant Pot to the "Sautee" mode. Add a serving of oil and brown your meat. On a Mediterranean diet, you could brown a leg of lamb or eisbein following a specific recipe. As you brown the meat, you can also add aromatics such as garlic, onion, or peppers to the pot.

Step 2: Once the meat has been browned, you will need to press the "Cancel" button. Proceed to press the "Manual" button followed by "Pressure." If you want to cook your meat dish in high-pressure mode, you will need to press the "Pressure" button again. Note that it is important to consult the given instructions on an Instant Pot recipe when setting the pressure so that your pot cooks the dish to perfection. Once the pressure has been set, use the plus and minus keys to set the cooking time.

Step 3: Place the glass lid on your Instant Pot and ensure that it is locked in place and doesn't jerk or shift. Your intelligent pot will also give you a warning sign when your lid hasn't been fastened on properly. Once it is locked-in, you should hear a sound informing you that the pot is ready to perform its magic.

Step 4: Ensure that the valve built into the lid is in the "Sealing" position.

Step 5: Your dish will only start cooking once the pot has generated enough pressure. A red button will pop up to inform you that the cooking process has begun. The Instant Pot will then begin a countdown until the cooking time has elapsed.

These steps will differ depending on your specific Mediterranean diet recipe, however, most recipes will follow a similar sequence. After the cooking time has lapsed and your meal is now ready to be served, you need to release the pressure from your Instant Pot. One way of releasing the pressure is by using the natural release method where you allow the valve on the lid to stay on the "Sealing" position until the pressure naturally dissipates over time. Depending on the meal you were cooking, it can take between 15 minutes to an hour for the pressure to fully dissipate. Generally, meals that contain minimal liquid (like a roast chicken) will take a shorter time releasing pressure than meals that contain a lot of liquid (like a soup or stew).

If you do not have the luxury of time, you can use the quick-release method to manually release pressure. To do this, you can carefully turn the valve to the "Venting" position and allow the steam to shoot out of it. As a safety precaution, use a kitchen tea towel or oven glove to turn the valve and ensure that your hands or fingers are never in contact with the valve or lid. When the pressure is released manually, it can reduce the amount of time you have to wait before serving your food. Foods with high-liquid content may still take up to 15 minutes to release all of the pressure. You can also opt to use the quick release method when your food has thoroughly cooked through and you don't want it to overcook as the pressure is being released naturally. Other times, you may want the food to continue cooking for a little while longer and therefore the natural release of pressure may be the best option for that particular recipe.

4 Tips Before You Begin Pressure-Cooking

If you are a newbie to using the Instant Pot, there are a few tips that you should remember along your journey:

1.Read-Through the Manual

I know that cooking with an Instant Pot is fun, however, it also requires a basic understanding of how the machine functions. Winging it is never advised when using an Instant Pot because not every model is built the same. Even the most experienced cook should read the user manual before preparing their first dish using an Instant Pot to avoid cooking disasters, burning food, careless cleaning, and caring for the pot.

2.Check On Your Detachable Power Cord

Sometimes you may notice that your turns pitch dark. This may be due to your Instant Pot experiencing a loose connection. Always check to see whether or not you have a detachable power cord. If you do, you may need to detach it from the base socket and reattach it again so that it is fitted properly to the base.

3.Don't Forget to Insert the Sealing Ring

The silicone sealing ring that comes as an accessory with your Instant Pot is a valuable component for effective pressure-cooking. Forgetting to insert the sealing ring may cause food to leak from the inner pot while cooking or a completely botched meal. Also, take time to ensure that it is securely put in place and doesn't have any cracks or leaks around its rim.

4.Don't Add Too Much Liquid

The saying goes, "no water, no pressure," however, when you add too much water you can sabotage your meal. Too much liquid added to your pot may cause your dish to become soggy. Your Instant Pot recipe should give you clear directions on the amount of water needed for the dish. Follow these guidelines to ensure that your food is not swimming in water.

CHAPTER 3

SOUPS AND STEWS

Gorgonzola and Broccoli Soup

Prep time: 10 minutes | Cook time: 30 minutes | Serves 4

- 8 ounces (227 g) Gorgonzola cheese, crumbled
- 1 cup broccoli, chopped
- 4 cups water
- 1 tablespoon olive oil
- ½ cup full-fat milk
- 1 tablespoon parsley, finely chopped
- ½ teaspoon salt
- ¼ teaspoon ground black pepper

1. Add all ingredients to the pot, seal the lid and cook on Soup/Broth mode for 30 minutes on High Pressure. Do a quick release. Remove the lid and sprinkle with fresh parsley. Serve warm.

Chickpea and Veg Stew

Prep time: 15 minutes | Cook time: 30 minutes | Serves 6 to 8

- ¼ cup extra-virgin olive oil, plus extra for drizzling
- 2 red bell peppers, stemmed, seeded, and cut into 1-inch pieces
- 1 onion, chopped fine
- ½ teaspoon table salt
- ½ teaspoon pepper
- 1½ tablespoons baharat
- 4 garlic cloves, minced
- 1 tablespoon tomato paste
- 4 cups vegetable or chicken broth
- 1 (28-ounce / 794-g) can whole peeled tomatoes, drained with juice reserved, chopped
- 1 pound (454 g) Yukon Gold potatoes, peeled and cut into ½-inch pieces
- 2 zucchini, quartered lengthwise and sliced 1 inch thick
- 1 (15-ounce / 425-g) can chickpeas, rinsed
- $^1/_3$ cup chopped fresh mint

1. Using highest Sauté function, heat oil in Instant Pot until shimmering. Add bell pepper, onion, salt, and pepper and cook until vegetables are softened and lightly browned, 5 to 7 minutes. Stir in baharat, garlic, and tomato paste and cook until fragrant, about 1 minute. Stir in broth and tomatoes and reserved juice, scraping up any browned bits, then stir in potatoes.
2. Lock lid in place and close pressure release valve. Select Manual function and cook for 9 minutes. Turn off Instant Pot and quick release pressure. Carefully remove lid, allowing steam to escape away from you.
3. Stir zucchini and chickpeas into stew and cook, using highest Sauté function, until zucchini is tender, 10 to 15 minutes. Turn off multicooker. Season with salt and pepper to taste. Drizzle individual portions with extra oil, and sprinkle with mint before serving.

Cannellini Bean and Spinach Stew

Prep time: 15 minutes | Cook time: 35 minutes | Serves 4

- 2 tablespoons olive oil
- 1 onion, chopped
- 2 cloves garlic, minced
- 2 carrots, peeled and chopped
- 1 cup celery, chopped
- 4 cups vegetable broth
- 1 cup cannellini beans, soaked,

drained, rinsed
- 1 teaspoon dried thyme
- 1 teaspoon dried rosemary
- 1 bay leaf
- 1 cup spinach, torn into pieces
- Salt and black pepper, to taste

1. Warm olive oil on Sauté. Stir in garlic and onion, and cook for 3 minutes until tender and fragrant. Mix in celery and carrots and cook for 2 to 3 minutes more until they start to soften. Add broth, bay leaf, thyme, rosemary, cannellini beans, and salt.
2. Seal the lid and cook for 30 minutes on High Pressure. Quick release the pressure and stir in spinach. Allow to sit for 2 to 4 minutes until the spinach wilts, and season with pepper and salt.

Shrimp and Potato Chowder

Prep time: 10 minutes | Cook time: 25 minutes | Serves 4

- 4 slices pancetta, chopped
- 4 tablespoons minced garlic
- 1 onion, chopped
- 2 potatoes, chopped
- 1 pound (454 g) canned corn kernels
- 4 cups vegetable stock
- 1 teaspoon dried rosemary
- 1 teaspoon salt
- 1 teaspoon black pepper
- 1 pound (454 g) jumbo shrimp, peeled, deveined
- 1 tablespoon olive oil
- ½ teaspoon red chili flakes
- ¾ cup heavy cream

1. Fry the pancetta for 5 minutes until crispy, on Sauté mode, and set aside. Add 2 tablespoons of garlic and onion, and stir-fry for 3 minutes. Add potatoes, corn, stock, rosemary, half of the salt, and pepper.
2. Seal the lid and cook on High Pressure for 10 minutes. Do a quick Pressure release. Remove to a serving bowl. In a bowl, toss the shrimp in the remaining garlic, salt, black pepper, olive oil, and flakes.
3. Wipe the pot clean and fry shrimp for 3-4 minutes per side, until pink. Mix in the heavy cream and cook for 2 minutes. Add shrimp to chowder, garnish with the reserved pancetta and serve immediately.

Chicken Leg and Chickpea Stew

- 1 pound (454 g) boneless, skinless chicken legs
- 2 teaspoons ground cumin
- ½ teaspoon cayenne pepper
- 2 tablespoons olive oil
- 1 onion, minced
- 2 jalapeño peppers, deseeded and minced
- 3 garlic cloves, crushed
- 2 teaspoons freshly grated ginger
- ¼ cup chicken stock
- 1 (24-ounce / 680-g) can crushed tomatoes
- 2 (14-ounce / 397-g) cans chickpeas, drained and rinsed
- Salt, to taste
- ½ cup coconut milk
- ¼ cup fresh parsley, chopped
- 2 cups hot cooked basmati rice

1. Season the chicken with 1 teaspoon salt, cayenne pepper, and cumin. Set on Sauté and warm the oil. Add jalapeño peppers, and onion, and cook for 5 minutes. Mix in ginger and garlic, and cook for 3 minutes until tender.
2. Add ¼ cup chicken stock into the cooker to ensure the pan is deglazed, from the pan's bottom scrape any browned bits of food. Mix the onion mixture with chickpeas, tomatoes, and salt. Stir in Seasoned chicken to coat in sauce.
3. Seal the lid and cook on High Pressure for 20 minutes. Release the pressure quickly. Remove the chicken and slice into chunks. Into the remaining sauce, mix in coconut milk; simmer for 5 minutes on Keep Warm. Split rice into 4 bowls. Top with chicken, then sauce and add cilantro for garnish.

Lamb and Potato Stew

- 1 pound (454 g) lamb neck, boneless
- 2 potatoes, peeled, cut into bite-sized pieces
- 2 large carrots, chopped
- 1 tomato, diced
- 1 small red bell pepper, chopped
- 1 garlic head, whole
- A handful of parsley, chopped
- ¼ cup lemon juice
- ½ teaspoon salt
- ½ teaspoon ground black pepper

1. Add the meat and season with salt. Add the remaining ingredients, tuck in one garlic head in the middle of the pot and add 2 cups of water. Add a handful of fresh parsley and seal the lid.
2. Cook on High Pressure for 45 minutes. When ready, do a quick release.

Beef and Green Bean Soup

Prep time: 10 minutes | Cook time: 30 minutes | Serves 3

- ½ pound (227 g) lean ground beef
- ½ tablespoon garlic, minced
- ½ tablespoon olive oil
- ½ medium onion, chopped
- 1 teaspoon dried thyme, crushed
- ½ teaspoon ground cumin
- 1½ cups fresh tomatoes, chopped finely
- ½ pound (227 g) fresh green beans, trimmed and cut into 1-inch pieces
- 2 cups low-sodium beef broth
- Freshly ground black pepper, to taste
- ⅛ cup Parmesan cheese, freshly grated

1. Select the Sauté function on your instant pot. Pour in the oil, add the beef, and cook for 5 minutes.
2. Add the thyme, cumin and garlic, then cook for 3 minutes.
3. Now stir in the beans, tomatoes and broth and secure the lid.
4. Set the Manual function to Low Pressure and cook for 20 minutes.
5. Quick release the pressure and remove the lid.
6. Drizzle some black pepper and Parmesan cheese on top.
7. Serve hot.

Turkey Meatball Soup

Prep time: 15 minutes | Cook time: 15 minutes | Serves 6 to 8

- 1 slice hearty white sandwich bread, torn into quarters
- ¼ cup whole milk
- 1 ounce (28 g) Manchego cheese, grated (½ cup), plus extra for serving
- 5 tablespoons minced fresh parsley, divided
- ½ teaspoon table salt
- 1 pound (454 g) ground turkey
- 1 tablespoon extra-virgin olive oil
- 1 onion, chopped
- 1 red bell pepper, stemmed, seeded, and cut into ¾-inch pieces
- 4 garlic cloves, minced
- 2 teaspoons smoked paprika
- ½ cup dry white wine
- 8 cups chicken broth
- 8 ounces (227 g) kale, stemmed and chopped

1. Using fork, mash bread and milk together into paste in large bowl. Stir in Manchego, 3 tablespoons parsley, and salt until combined. Add turkey and knead mixture with your hands until well combined. Pinch off and roll 2-teaspoon-size pieces of mixture into balls and arrange on large plate (you should have about 35 meatballs); set aside.

2. Using highest Sauté function, heat oil in Instant Pot until shimmering. Add onion and bell pepper and cook until softened and lightly browned, 5 to 7 minutes. Stir in garlic and paprika and cook until fragrant, about 30 seconds. Stir in wine, scraping up any browned bits, and cook until almost completely evaporated, about 5 minutes. Stir in broth and kale, then gently submerge meatballs.
3. Lock lid in place and close pressure release valve. Select Manual function and cook for 3 minutes. Turn off Instant Pot and quick release pressure. Carefully remove lid, allowing steam to escape away from you.
4. Stir in remaining 2 tablespoons parsley and season with salt and pepper to taste. Serve, passing extra Manchego separately.

Spiced Carrot Soup

Prep time: 15 minutes | Cook time: 10 minutes | Serves 6 to 8

- 2 tablespoons extra-virgin olive oil
- 2 onions, chopped
- 1 teaspoon table salt
- 1 tablespoon grated fresh ginger
- 1 tablespoon ground coriander
- 1 tablespoon ground fennel
- 1 teaspoon ground cinnamon
- 4 cups vegetable or chicken broth
- 2 cups water
- 2 pounds (907 g) carrots, peeled
- and cut into 2-inch pieces
- ½ teaspoon baking soda
- 2 tablespoons pomegranate molasses
- ½ cup plain Greek yogurt
- ½ cup hazelnuts, toasted, skinned, and chopped
- ½ cup chopped fresh cilantro or mint

1. Using highest Sauté function, heat oil in Instant Pot until shimmering. Add onions and salt and cook until onions are softened, about 5 minutes. Stir in ginger, coriander, fennel, and cinnamon and cook until fragrant, about 30 seconds. Stir in broth, water, carrots, and baking soda.
2. Lock lid in place and close pressure release valve. Select Manual function and cook for 3 minutes. Turn off Instant Pot and quick release pressure. Carefully remove lid, allowing steam to escape away from you.
3. Working in batches, process soup in blender until smooth, 1 to 2 minutes. Return processed soup to Instant Pot and bring to simmer using highest Sauté function. Season with salt and pepper to taste. Drizzle individual portions with pomegranate molasses and top with yogurt, hazelnuts, and cilantro before serving.

Italian Beef and Vegetable Stew

Prep time: 20 minutes | Cook time: 50 minutes | Serves 6

- ¼ cup flour
- 2 teaspoons salt
- 1 teaspoon paprika
- 1 teaspoon ground black pepper
- 2 pounds (907 g) beef chuck, cubed
- 4 tablespoons olive oil
- 1 onion, diced
- 3 garlic cloves, minced
- 1 cup dry red wine
- 2 cups beef stock
- 1 tablespoon dried Italian seasoning
- 2 teaspoons Worcestershire sauce
- 4 cups potatoes, diced
- 2 celery stalks, chopped
- 3 cups carrots, chopped
- 3 tomatoes, chopped
- 2 bell peppers, thinly chopped
- Salt and ground black pepper to taste
- A handful of fresh parsley, chopped

1. In a bowl, mix black pepper, beef, flour, paprika, and 1 teaspoon salt. Toss the ingredients and ensure the beef is well-coated. Warm oil on Sauté mode. Add beef and cook for 8 to 10 minutes until browned. Set aside.
2. To the same fat, add garlic, onion, and celery, bell peppers, and cook for 4 to 5 minutes until tender.
3. Deglaze with wine, scrape the bottom to get rid of any browned beef bits. Pour in remaining salt, beef stock, Worcestershire sauce, and Italian seasoning.
4. Return beef to the pot; add carrots, tomatoes, and potatoes. Seal the lid, press Meat/Stew and cook on High Pressure for 35 minutes. Release pressure naturally for 10 minutes. Taste and adjust the seasonings as necessary. Serve on plates and scatter over the parsley.

Pumpkin and Beef Stew

Prep time: 15 minutes | Cook time: 25 minutes | Serves 6

- 2 tablespoons canola oil
- 2 pounds (907 g) stew beef, cut into 1-inch chunks
- 1 cup red wine
- 1 onion, chopped
- 1 teaspoon garlic powder
- 1 teaspoon salt
- 3 whole cloves
- 1 bay leaf
- 3 carrots, chopped
- ½ butternut pumpkin, chopped
- 2 tablespoons cornstarch
- 3 tablespoons water

1. Warm oil on Sauté mode. Brown the beef for 5 minutes on each side.
2. Deglaze the pot with wine, scrape the bottom to get rid of any browned beef bits. Add onion, salt, bay leaf, cloves, and garlic powder. Seal the lid, press Meat/Stew and cook on High for 15 minutes.
3. Release the pressure quickly. Add pumpkin and carrots without stirring.
4. Seal the lid and cook on High Pressure for 5 minutes. Release the pressure quickly.
5. In a bowl, mix water and cornstarch until cornstarch dissolves completely; mix into the stew. Allow the stew to simmer while uncovered on Keep Warm for 5 minutes until you attain the desired thickness.

Moroccan Lamb and Lentil Soup

Prep time: 15 minutes | Cook time: 30 minutes | Serves 6 to 8

- 1 pound (454 g) lamb shoulder chops (blade or round bone), 1 to 1½ inches thick, trimmed and halved
- ¾ teaspoon table salt, divided
- ⅛ teaspoon pepper
- 1 tablespoon extra-virgin olive oil
- 1 onion, chopped fine
- ¼ cup harissa, plus extra for serving
- 1 tablespoon all-purpose flour
- 8 cups chicken broth
- 1 cup French green lentils, picked over and rinsed
- 1 (15-ounce / 425-g) can chickpeas, rinsed
- 2 tomatoes, cored and cut into ¼-inch pieces
- ½ cup chopped fresh cilantro

1. Pat lamb dry with paper towels and sprinkle with ¼ teaspoon salt and pepper. Using highest Sauté function, heat oil in Instant Pot for 5 minutes (or until just smoking). Place lamb in pot and cook until well browned on first side, about 4 minutes; transfer to plate.
2. Add onion and remaining ½ teaspoon salt to fat left in pot and cook, using highest Sauté function, until softened, about 5 minutes. Stir in harissa and flour and cook until fragrant, about 30 seconds. Slowly whisk in broth, scraping up any browned bits and smoothing out any lumps. Stir in lentils, then nestle lamb into multicooker and add any accumulated juices.
3. Lock lid in place and close pressure release valve. Select Manual function and cook for 10 minutes. Turn off Instant Pot and quick release pressure. Carefully remove lid, allowing steam to escape away from you.
4. Transfer lamb to cutting board, let cool slightly, then shred into bite-size pieces using 2 forks; discard excess fat and bones. Stir lamb and chickpeas into soup and let sit until heated through, about 3 minutes. Season with salt and pepper to taste. Top individual portions with tomatoes and sprinkle with cilantro. Serve, passing extra harissa separately.

Sicilian Swordfish Stew

- 2 tablespoons extra-virgin olive oil
- 2 onions, chopped fine
- 1 teaspoon table salt
- ½ teaspoon pepper
- 1 teaspoon minced fresh thyme or ¼ teaspoon dried
- Pinch red pepper flakes
- 4 garlic cloves, minced, divided
- 1 (28-ounce / 794-g) can whole peeled tomatoes, drained with juice reserved, chopped coarse
- 1 (8-ounce / 227-g) bottle clam juice
- ¼ cup dry white wine
- ¼ cup golden raisins
- 2 tablespoons capers, rinsed
- 1½ pounds (680 g) skinless swordfish steak, 1 to 1½ inches thick, cut into 1-inch pieces
- ¼ cup pine nuts, toasted
- ¼ cup minced fresh mint
- 1 teaspoon grated orange zest

1. Using highest Sauté function, heat oil in Instant Pot until shimmering. Add onions, salt, and pepper and cook until onions are softened, about 5 minutes. Stir in thyme, pepper flakes, and three-quarters of garlic and cook until fragrant, about 30 seconds. Stir in tomatoes and reserved juice, clam juice, wine, raisins, and capers. Nestle swordfish into pot and spoon some cooking liquid over top.
2. Lock lid in place and close pressure release valve. Select Manual function and cook for 1 minute. Turn off Instant Pot and quick release pressure. Carefully remove lid, allowing steam to escape away from you.
3. Combine pine nuts, mint, orange zest, and remaining garlic in bowl. Season stew with salt and pepper to taste. Sprinkle individual portions with pine nut mixture before serving.

Leek and Farro Soup

- 1 cup whole farro
- 1 tablespoon extra-virgin olive oil, plus extra for drizzling
- 3 ounces (85 g) pancetta, chopped fine
- 1 pound (454 g) leeks, ends trimmed, chopped, and washed thoroughly
- 2 carrots, peeled and chopped
- 1 celery rib, chopped
- 8 cups chicken broth, plus extra as needed
- ½ cup minced fresh parsley
- Grated Parmesan cheese

1. Pulse farro in blender until about half of grains are broken into smaller pieces, about 6 pulses; set aside.
2. Using highest Sauté function, heat oil in Instant Pot until shimmering. Add pancetta and cook until lightly browned, 3 to 5 minutes. Stir in leeks, carrots, and celery and cook until softened, about 5 minutes. Stir in broth, scraping up any browned bits, then stir in farro.
3. Lock lid in place and close pressure release valve. Select Manual function and cook for 8 minutes. Turn off Instant Pot and quick release pressure. Carefully remove lid, allowing steam to escape away from you.
4. Adjust consistency with extra hot broth as needed. Stir in parsley and season with salt and pepper to taste. Drizzle individual portions with extra oil and top with Parmesan before serving.

Gigante Bean Soup

Prep time: 15 minutes | Cook time: 15 minutes | Serves 6 to 8

- 1½ tablespoons table salt, for brining
- 1 pound (454 g) dried gigante beans, picked over and rinsed
- 2 tablespoons extra-virgin olive oil, plus extra for drizzling
- 5 celery ribs, cut into ½-inch pieces, plus ½ cup leaves, minced
- 1 onion, chopped
- ½ teaspoon table salt

- 4 garlic cloves, minced
- 4 cups vegetable or chicken broth
- 4 cups water
- 2 bay leaves
- ½ cup pitted kalamata olives, chopped
- 2 tablespoons minced fresh marjoram or oregano
- Lemon wedges

1. Dissolve 1½ tablespoons salt in 2 quarts cold water in large container. Add beans and soak at room temperature for at least 8 hours or up to 24 hours. Drain and rinse well.
2. Using highest Sauté function, heat oil in Instant Pot until shimmering. Add celery pieces, onion, and ½ teaspoon salt and cook until vegetables are softened, about 5 minutes. Stir in garlic and cook until fragrant, about 30 seconds. Stir in broth, water, beans, and bay leaves.
3. Lock lid in place and close pressure release valve. Select Manual function and cook for 6 minutes. Turn off Instant Pot and let pressure release naturally for 15 minutes. Quick release any remaining pressure, then carefully remove lid, allowing steam to escape away from you.
4. Combine celery leaves, olives, and marjoram in bowl. Discard bay leaves. Season soup with salt and pepper to taste. Top individual portions with celery-olive mixture and drizzle with extra oil. Serve with lemon wedges.

Chicken, Squas, and Chickpea Soup

Prep time: 15 minutes | Cook time: 30 minutes | Serves 6 to 8

- 2 tablespoons extra-virgin olive oil
- 1 onion, chopped
- 1¾ teaspoons table salt
- 2 tablespoons tomato paste
- 4 garlic cloves, minced
- 1 tablespoon ground coriander
- 1½ teaspoons ground cumin
- 1 teaspoon ground cardamom
- ½ teaspoon ground allspice
- ¼ teaspoon cayenne pepper
- 7 cups water, divided
- 2 (12-ounce / 340-g) bone-in split chicken breasts, trimmed
- 4 (5- to 7-ounce / 142- to 198-g) bone-in chicken thighs, trimmed
- 1½ pounds (680 g) butternut squash, peeled, seeded, and cut into 1½-inch pieces (4 cups)
- 1 (15-ounce / 425-g) can chickpeas, rinsed
- ½ cup chopped fresh cilantro

1. Using highest Sauté function, heat oil in Instant Pot until shimmering. Add onion and salt and cook until onion is softened, about 5 minutes. Stir in tomato paste, garlic, coriander, cumin, cardamom, allspice, and cayenne and cook until fragrant, about 30 seconds. Stir in 5 cups water, scraping up any browned bits. Nestle chicken breasts and thighs in pot, then arrange squash evenly around chicken.
2. Lock lid in place and close pressure release valve. Select Manual function and cook for 20 minutes. Turn off Instant Pot and quick release pressure. Carefully remove lid, allowing steam to escape away from you.
3. Transfer chicken to cutting board, let cool slightly, then shred into bite-size pieces using 2 forks; discard skin and bones.
4. Using wide, shallow spoon, skim excess fat from surface of soup, then break squash into bite-size pieces. Stir chicken and any accumulated juices, chickpeas, and remaining 2 cups water into soup and let sit until heated through, about 3 minutes. Stir in cilantro and season with salt and pepper to taste. Serve.

Beef, Eggplant, and Potato Stew

- 2 pounds (907 g) boneless short ribs, trimmed and cut into 1-inch pieces
- 1½ teaspoons table salt, divided
- 2 tablespoons extra-virgin olive oil
- 1 onion, chopped fine
- 3 tablespoons tomato paste
- ¼ cup all-purpose flour
- 3 garlic cloves, minced
- 1 tablespoon ground cumin
- 1 teaspoon ground turmeric
- 1 teaspoon ground cardamom
- ¾ teaspoon ground cinnamon
- 4 cups chicken broth
- 1 cup water
- 1 pound (454 g) eggplant, cut into 1-inch pieces
- 1 pound (454 g) Yukon Gold potatoes, unpeeled, cut into 1-inch pieces
- ½ cup chopped fresh mint or parsley

1. Pat beef dry with paper towels and sprinkle with 1 teaspoon salt. Using highest Sauté function, heat oil in Instant Pot for 5 minutes (or until just smoking). Brown half of beef on all sides, 7 to 9 minutes; transfer to bowl. Set aside remaining uncooked beef.
2. Add onion to fat left in pot and cook, using highest Sauté function, until softened, about 5 minutes. Stir in tomato paste, flour, garlic, cumin, turmeric, cardamom, cinnamon, and remaining ½ teaspoon salt. Cook until fragrant, about 1 minute. Slowly whisk in broth and water, scraping up any browned bits. Stir in eggplant and potatoes. Nestle remaining uncooked beef into pot along with browned beef, and add any accumulated juices.
3. Lock lid in place and close pressure release valve. Select Manual function and cook for 30 minutes. Turn off Instant Pot and quick release pressure. Carefully remove lid, allowing steam to escape away from you.
4. Using wide, shallow spoon, skim excess fat from surface of stew. Stir in mint and season with salt and pepper to taste. Serve.

Provençal Chicken and Anchovy Soup

- 1 tablespoon extra-virgin olive oil
- 2 fennel bulbs, 2 tablespoons fronds minced, stalks discarded, bulbs halved, cored, and cut into ½-inch pieces
- 1 onion, chopped
- 1¾ teaspoons table salt
- 2 tablespoons tomato paste
- 4 garlic cloves, minced
- 1 tablespoon minced fresh thyme or 1 teaspoon dried
- 2 anchovy fillets, minced
- 7 cups water, divided
- 1 (14.5-ounce / 411-g) can diced tomatoes, drained
- 2 carrots, peeled, halved lengthwise, and sliced ½ inch thick
- 2 (12-ounce / 340-g) bone-in split chicken breasts, trimmed
- 4 (5- to 7-ounce / 142- to 198-g) bone-in chicken thighs, trimmed
- ½ cup pitted brine-cured green olives, chopped
- 1 teaspoon grated orange zest

1. Using highest Sauté function, heat oil in Instant Pot until shimmering. Add fennel pieces, onion, and salt and cook until vegetables are softened, about 5 minutes. Stir in tomato paste, garlic, thyme, and anchovies and cook until fragrant, about 30 seconds. Stir in 5 cups water, scraping up any browned bits, then stir in tomatoes and carrots. Nestle chicken breasts and thighs in pot.
2. Lock lid in place and close pressure release valve. Select Manual function and cook for 20 minutes. Turn off Instant Pot and quick release pressure. Carefully remove lid, allowing steam to escape away from you.
3. Transfer chicken to cutting board, let cool slightly, then shred into bite-size pieces using 2 forks; discard skin and bones.
4. Using wide, shallow spoon, skim excess fat from surface of soup. Stir chicken and any accumulated juices, olives, and remaining 2 cups water into soup and let sit until heated through, about 3 minutes. Stir in fennel fronds and orange zest, and season with salt and pepper to taste. Serve.

Cannellini Bean and Escarole Soup

Prep time: 15 minutes | Cook time: 15 minutes | Serves 6 to 8

- 1½ tablespoons table salt, for brining
- 1 pound (454 g) dried cannellini beans, picked over and rinsed
- 1 large onion, chopped coarse
- 2 celery ribs, chopped coarse
- 4 garlic cloves, peeled
- 1 (28-ounce / 794-g) can whole peeled tomatoes
- 2 tablespoons extra-virgin olive oil, plus extra for drizzling
- 1 fennel bulb, stalks discarded, bulb halved, cored, and cut into ½-inch pieces
- ½ teaspoon table salt
- ⅛ teaspoon red pepper flakes
- 8 cups chicken broth
- 1 small head escarole, trimmed and cut into ½-inch pieces (8 cups)
- 2 large egg yolks
- ½ cup chopped fresh parsley
- 1 tablespoon minced fresh oregano
- Grated Pecorino Romano cheese
- Lemon wedges

1. Dissolve 1½ tablespoons salt in 2 quarts cold water in large container. Add beans and soak at room temperature for at least 8 hours or up to 24 hours. Drain and rinse well.
2. Pulse onion, celery, and garlic in food processor until very finely chopped, 15 to 20 pulses, scraping down sides of bowl as needed; set aside. Add tomatoes and their juice to now-empty processor and pulse until tomatoes are finely chopped, 10 to 12 pulses; set aside.
3. Using highest Sauté function, heat oil in Instant Pot until shimmering. Add onion mixture, fennel, ½ teaspoon salt, and pepper flakes and cook until fennel begins to soften, 7 to 9 minutes. Stir in broth, tomatoes, and beans.
4. Lock lid in place and close pressure release valve. Select Manual function and cook for 1 minute. Turn off Instant Pot and let pressure release naturally for 15 minutes. Quick release any remaining pressure, then carefully remove lid, allowing steam to escape away from you.
5. Measure out and reserve 1 cup hot broth. Stir escarole into multicooker, 1 handful at a time, and let cook in residual heat until escarole is wilted, about 5 minutes.
6. Gently whisk egg yolks together in small bowl. Whisking constantly, slowly add reserved broth to eggs until combined. Stir yolk mixture, parsley, and oregano into soup. Season with salt and pepper to taste. Top individual portions with Pecorino and drizzle with extra oil. Serve with lemon wedges.

Oxtail and Veggie Soup

- 4 pounds (1.8 kg) oxtails, trimmed
- 1 teaspoon table salt
- 1 tablespoon extra-virgin olive oil
- 1 onion, chopped fine
- 2 carrots, peeled and chopped fine
- ¼ cup ground dried Aleppo pepper
- 6 garlic cloves, minced
- 2 tablespoons tomato paste
- ¾ teaspoon dried oregano
- ½ teaspoon ground cinnamon
- ½ teaspoon ground cumin
- 6 cups water
- 1 (28-ounce / 794-g) can diced tomatoes, drained
- 1 (15-ounce / 425-g) can navy beans, rinsed
- 1 tablespoon sherry vinegar
- ¼ cup chopped fresh parsley
- ½ preserved lemon, pulp and white pith removed, rind rinsed and minced (2 tablespoons)

1. Pat oxtails dry with paper towels and sprinkle with salt. Using highest Sauté function, heat oil in Instant Pot for 5 minutes (or until just smoking). Brown half of oxtails, 4 to 6 minutes per side; transfer to plate. Set aside remaining uncooked oxtails.
2. Add onion and carrots to fat left in pot and cook, using highest Sauté function, until softened, about 5 minutes. Stir in Aleppo pepper, garlic, tomato paste, oregano, cinnamon, and cumin and cook until fragrant, about 30 seconds. Stir in water, scraping up any browned bits, then stir in tomatoes. Nestle remaining uncooked oxtails into pot along with browned oxtails and add any accumulated juices.
3. Lock lid in place and close pressure release valve. Select Manual function and cook for 45 minutes. Turn off Instant Pot and quick release pressure. Carefully remove lid, allowing steam to escape away from you.
4. Transfer oxtails to cutting board, let cool slightly, then shred into bite-size pieces using 2 forks; discard bones and excess fat. Strain broth through fine-mesh strainer into large container; return solids to now-empty pot. Using wide, shallow spoon, skim excess fat from surface of liquid; return to pot.
5. Stir shredded oxtails and any accumulated juices and beans into pot. Using highest Sauté function, cook until soup is heated through, about 5 minutes. Stir in vinegar and parsley and season with salt and pepper to taste. Serve, passing preserved lemon separately.

CHAPTER 4

GRAINS, BEANS, AND PASTA

Shrimp and Asparagus Risotto

Prep time: 15 minutes | Cook time: 58 minutes | Serves 4

- 1 tablespoon olive oil
- 1 pound (454 g) asparagus, trimmed and roughly chopped
- 1 cup spinach, chopped
- 1½ cups mushrooms, chopped
- 1 cup rice, rinsed and drained
- 1¼ cups chicken broth
- ¾ cup milk
- 1 tablespoon coconut oil
- 16 shrimp, cleaned and deveined
- Salt and ground black pepper, to taste
- ¾ cup Parmesan cheese, shredded

1. Warm the oil on Sauté. Add spinach, mushrooms and asparagus and Sauté for 10 minutes until cooked through. Press Cancel. Add rice, milk and chicken broth to the pot as you stir.
2. Seal the lid, press Multigrain and cook for 40 minutes on High Pressure. Do a quick release, open the lid and put the rice on a serving plate.
3. Take back the empty pot to the pressure cooker, add coconut oil and press Sauté. Add shrimp and cook each side for 4 minutes until cooked through and turns pink. Set shrimp over rice, add pepper and salt for seasoning. Serve topped with shredded Parmesan cheese.

Pancetta with Garbanzo Beans

Prep time: 10 minutes | Cook time: 38 minutes | Serves 6

- 3 strips pancetta
- 1 onion, diced
- 15 ounces (425 g) canned garbanzo beans
- 2 cups water
- 1 cup apple cider
- 2 garlic cloves, minced
- ½ cup ketchup
- ¼ cup sugar
- 1 teaspoon ground mustard powder
- 1 teaspoon salt
- 1 teaspoon black pepper
- Fresh parsley, for garnish

1. Cook pancetta for 5 minutes, until crispy, on Sauté mode. Add onion and garlic, and cook for 3 minutes until soft. Mix in garbanzo beans, ketchup, sugar, salt, apple cider, mustard powder, water, and pepper.
2. Seal the lid, press Bean/Chili and cook on High Pressure for 30 minutes. Release pressure naturally for 10 minutes. Serve in bowls garnished with parsley.

Brown Rice Stuffed Portobello Mushrooms

Prep time: 15 minutes | Cook time: 10 minutes | Serves 4

- 4 large portobello mushrooms, stems and gills removed
- 2 tablespoons olive oil
- ½ cup brown rice, cooked
- 1 tomato, seed removed and chopped
- ¼ cup black olives, pitted and chopped
- 1 green bell pepper, seeded and diced
- ½ cup feta cheese, crumbled
- Juice of 1 lemon
- ½ teaspoon salt
- ½ teaspoon ground black pepper
- Minced fresh cilantro, for garnish
- 1 cup vegetable broth

1. Brush the mushrooms with olive oil. Arrange the mushrooms in a single layer in an oiled baking pan. In a bowl, mix the rice, tomato, olives, bell pepper, feta cheese, lemon juice, salt, and black pepper.
2. Spoon the rice mixture into the mushrooms. Pour in the broth, seal the lid and cook on High Pressure for 10 minutes. Do a quick release. Garnish with fresh cilantro and serve immediately.

Roasted Butternut Squash and Rice

Prep time: 15 minutes | Cook time: 15 minutes | Serves 4

- ½ cup water
- 2 cups vegetable broth
- 1 small butternut squash, peeled and sliced
- 2 tablespoons olive oil, divided
- 1 teaspoon salt
- 1 teaspoon freshly ground black pepper
- 1 cup feta cheese, cubed
- 1 tablespoon coconut aminos
- 2 teaspoons arrowroot starch
- 1 cup jasmine rice, cooked

1. Pour the rice and broth in the pot and stir to combine. In a bowl, toss butternut squash with 1 tablespoon of olive oil and season with salt and black pepper.
2. In another bowl, mix the remaining olive oil, water and coconut aminos. Toss feta in the mixture, add the arrowroot starch, and toss again to combine well. Transfer to a greased baking dish.
3. Lay a trivet over the rice and place the baking dish on the trivet. Seal the lid and cook on High for 15 minutes. Do a quick pressure release. Fluff the rice with a fork and serve with squash and feta.

Rice and Sweet Potato Pilaf

- 2 tablespoons extra-virgin olive oil
- 1 onion, chopped fine
- ½ teaspoon table salt
- 2 garlic cloves, minced
- 1½ teaspoons ground turmeric
- 1 teaspoon ground coriander
- ⅛ teaspoon cayenne pepper
- 2 cups chicken broth
- 1½ cups long-grain white rice, rinsed
- 12 ounces (340 g) sweet potato, peeled, quartered lengthwise, and sliced ½ inch thick
- ½ preserved lemon, pulp and white pith removed, rind rinsed and minced (2 tablespoons)
- ½ cup shelled pistachios, toasted and chopped
- ¼ cup fresh cilantro leaves
- ¼ cup pomegranate seeds

1. Using highest Sauté function, heat oil in Instant Pot until shimmering. Add onion and salt and cook until onion is softened, about 5 minutes. Stir in garlic, turmeric, coriander, and cayenne and cook until fragrant, about 30 seconds. Stir in broth, rice, and sweet potato.
2. Lock lid in place and close pressure release valve. Select Manual function and cook for 4 minutes. Turn off Instant Pot and quick release pressure. Carefully remove lid, allowing steam to escape away from you.
3. Add preserved lemon and gently fluff rice with fork to combine. Lay clean dish towel over pot, replace lid, and let sit for 5 minutes. Season with salt and pepper to taste. Transfer to serving dish and sprinkle with pistachios, cilantro, and pomegranate seeds. Serve.

Carrot Risoni

- 1 cup orzo, rinsed
- 2 cups water
- 2 carrots, cut into sticks
- 1 large onion, chopped
- 2 tablespoons olive oil
- Salt, to taste
- Fresh cilantro, chopped, for garnish

1. Heat oil on Sauté. Add onion and carrots and stir-fry for about 10 minutes until tender and crispy. Remove to a plate and set aside. Add water, salt and orzo in the instant pot.
2. Seal the lid and cook on High Pressure for 1 minute. Do a quick release. Fluff the cooked orzo with a fork. Transfer to a serving plate and top with the carrots and onion. Serve scattered with cilantro.

Grana Padano Risotto

- 2 tablespoons olive oil
- 1 white onion, chopped
- 2 cups Carnaroli rice, rinsed
- ¼ cup dry white wine
- 4 cups chicken stock
- 1 teaspoon salt
- ½ teaspoon ground white pepper
- 2 tablespoons Grana padano cheese, grated
- ¼ tablespoon Grana padano cheese, flakes

1. Warm oil on Sauté. Stir-fry onion for 3 minutes until soft and translucent. Add rice and cook for 5 minutes stirring occasionally.
2. Pour wine into the pot to deglaze, scrape away any browned bits of food from the pan.
3. Stir in stock, pepper, and salt to the pot. Seal the lid, press Rice and cook on High Pressure for 15 minutes. Release the pressure quickly.
4. Sprinkle with grated Parmesan cheese and stir well. Top with flaked cheese for garnish before serving.

Pesto Arborio Rice and Veggie Bowls

- 1 cup arborio rice, rinsed and drained
- 2 cups vegetable broth
- Salt and black pepper to taste
- 1 potato, peeled, cubed
- 1 head broccoli, cut into small florets
- 1 bunch baby carrots, peeled
- ¼ cabbage, chopped
- 2 eggs
- ¼ cup pesto sauce
- Lemon wedges, for serving

1. In the pot, mix broth, pepper, rice and salt. Set trivet to the inner pot on top of rice and add a steamer basket to the top of the trivet. Mix carrots, potato, eggs and broccoli in the steamer basket. Add pepper and salt for seasoning.
2. Seal the lid and cook for 1 minute on High Pressure. Quick release the pressure.
3. Take away the trivet and steamer basket from the pot. Set the eggs in a bowl of ice water. Then peel and halve the eggs. Use a fork to fluff rice. Adjust the seasonings.
4. In two bowls, equally divide rice, broccoli, eggs, carrots, sweet potatoes, and a dollop of pesto. Serve alongside a lemon wedge.

Caprese Fusilli

Prep time: 15 minutes | Cook time: 7 minutes | Serves 3

- 1 tablespoon olive oil
- 1 onion, thinly chopped
- 6 garlic cloves, minced
- 1 teaspoon red pepper flakes
- 2½ cups dried fusilli
- 1 (15-ounce / 425-g) can tomato sauce
- 1 cup tomatoes, halved
- 1 cup water
- ¼ cup basil leaves
- 1 teaspoon salt
- 1 cup Ricotta cheese, crumbled
- 2 tablespoons chopped fresh basil

1. Warm oil on Sauté. Add red pepper flakes, garlic and onion and cook for 3 minutes until soft.
2. Mix in fusilli, tomatoes, half of the basil leaves, water, tomato sauce, and salt. Seal the lid, and cook on High Pressure for 4 minutes. Release the pressure quickly.
3. Transfer the pasta to a serving platter and top with the crumbled ricotta and remaining chopped basil.

Beef and Bean Stuffed Pasta Shells

Prep time: 15 minutes | Cook time: 17 minutes | Serves 4

- 2 tablespoons olive oil
- 1 pound (454 g) ground beef
- 1 pound (454 g) pasta shells
- 2 cups water
- 15 ounces (425 g) tomato sauce
- 1 (15-ounce / 425-g) can black beans, drained and rinsed
- 15 ounces (425 g) canned corn, drained (or 2 cups frozen corn)
- 10 ounces (283 g) red enchilada sauce
- 4 ounces (113 g) diced green chiles
- 1 cup shredded Mozzarella cheese
- Salt and ground black pepper to taste
- Additional cheese for topping
- Finely chopped parsley for garnish

1. Heat oil on Sauté. Add ground beef and cook for 7 minutes until it starts to brown.
2. Mix in pasta, tomato sauce, enchilada sauce, black beans, water, corn, and green chiles and stir to coat well. Add more water if desired.
3. Seal the lid and cook on High Pressure for 10 minutes. Do a quick Pressure release. Into the pasta mixture, mix in Mozzarella cheese until melted; add black pepper and salt. Garnish with parsley to serve.

Chili Halloumi Cheese with Rice

- 2 cups water
- 2 tablespoons brown sugar
- 2 tablespoons rice vinegar
- 1 tablespoon sweet chili sauce
- 1 tablespoon olive oil
- 1 teaspoon fresh minced garlic

- 20 ounces (567 g) Halloumi cheese, cubed
- 1 cup rice
- ¼ cup chopped fresh chives, for garnish

1. Heat the oil on Sauté and fry the halloumi for 5 minutes until golden brown. Set aside.
2. To the pot, add water, garlic, olive oil, vinegar, sugar, soy sauce, and chili sauce and mix well until smooth. Stir in rice noodles. Seal the lid and cook on High Pressure for 3 minutes. Release the pressure quickly. Split the rice between bowls. Top with fried halloumi and sprinkle with fresh chives before serving.

Parmesan Squash Linguine

- 1 cup flour
- 2 teaspoons salt
- 2 eggs
- 4 cups water
- 1 cup seasoned breadcrumbs
- ½ cup grated Parmesan cheese, plus more for garnish

- 1 yellow squash, peeled and sliced
- 1 pound (454 g) linguine
- 24 ounces (680 g) canned Seasoned tomato sauce
- 2 tablespoons olive oil
- 1 cup shredded Mozzarella cheese
- Minced fresh basil, for garnish

1. Break the linguine in half. Put it in the pot and add water and half of salt. Seal the lid and cook on High Pressure for 5 minutes. Combine the flour and 1 teaspoon of salt in a bowl. In another bowl, whisk the eggs and 2 tablespoons of water. In a third bowl, mix the breadcrumbs and Mozzarella cheese.
2. Coat each squash slices in the flour. Shake off excess flour, dip in the egg wash, and dredge in the bread crumbs. Set aside. Quickly release the pressure. Remove linguine to a serving bowl and mix in the tomato sauce and sprinkle with fresh basil. Heat oil on Sauté and fry breaded squash until crispy.
3. Serve the squash topped Mozzarella cheese with the linguine on side.

Rice and Bean Stuffed Zucchini

- 2 small zucchini, halved lengthwise
- ½ cup cooked rice
- ½ cup canned white beans, drained and rinsed
- ½ cup chopped tomatoes
- ½ cup chopped toasted cashew nuts
- ½ cup grated Parmesan cheese
- 2 tablespoons olive oil, divided
- ½ teaspoon salt
- ½ teaspoon freshly ground black pepper

1. Pour 1 cup of water in the instant pot and insert a trivet. Scoop out the pulp of zucchini and chop roughly.
2. In a bowl, mix the zucchini pulp, rice, tomatoes, cashew nuts, ¼ cup of Parmesan, 1 tablespoon of olive oil, salt, and black pepper. Fill the zucchini boats with the mixture, and arrange the stuffed boats in a single layer on the trivet. Seal the lid and cook for 15 minutes on Steam on High. Do a quick release and serve.

Rigatoni and Zucchini Minestrone

- 3 tablespoons olive oil
- 1 onion, diced
- 1 celery stalk, diced
- 1 large carrot, peeled and diced
- 14 ounces (397 g) canned chopped tomatoes
- 4 ounces (113 g) rigatoni
- 3 cups water
- 1 cup chopped zucchini
- 1 bay leaf
- 1 teaspoon mixed herbs
- ¼ teaspoon cayenne pepper
- ½ teaspoon salt
- ¼ cup shredded Pecorino Romano cheese
- 1 garlic clove, minced
- $1/3$ cup olive oil based pesto

1. Heat oil on Sauté and cook onion, celery, garlic, and carrot for 3 minutes, stirring occasionally until the vegetables are softened. Stir in rigatoni, tomatoes, water, zucchini, bay leaf, herbs, cayenne, and salt.
2. Seal the lid and cook on High for 4 minutes. Do a natural pressure release for 5 minutes. Adjust the taste of the soup with salt and black pepper, and remove the bay leaf.
3. Ladle the soup into serving bowls and drizzle the pesto over. Serve with the garlic toasts.

Pork and Spinach Spaghetti

Prep time: 15 minutes | Cook time: 16 minutes | Serves 4

- 2 tablespoons olive oil
- ½ cup onion, chopped
- 1 garlic clove, minced
- 1 pound (454 g) ground pork
- 2 cups water
- 1 (14-ounce / 397-g) can diced tomatoes, drained
- ½ cup sun-dried tomatoes
- 1 tablespoon dried oregano
- 1 teaspoon Italian seasoning
- 1 fresh jalapeño chile, stemmed, seeded, and minced
- 1 teaspoon salt
- 8 ounces (227 g) dried spaghetti, halved
- 1 cup spinach

1. Warm oil on Sauté. Add onion and garlic and cook for 2 minutes until softened. Stir in pork and cook for 5 minutes. Stir in jalapeño, water, sun-dried tomatoes, Italian seasoning, oregano, diced tomatoes, and salt with the chicken; mix spaghetti and press to submerge into the sauce.
2. Seal the lid and cook on High Pressure for 9 minutes. Release the pressure quickly. Stir in spinach, close lid again, and simmer on Keep Warm for 5 minutes until spinach is wilted.

Cheesy Tomato Linguine

Prep time: 15 minutes | Cook time: 11 minutes | Serves 4

- 2 tablespoons olive oil
- 1 small onion, diced
- 2 garlic cloves, minced
- 1 cup cherry tomatoes, halved
- 1½ cups vegetable stock
- ¼ cup julienned basil leaves
- 1 teaspoon salt
- ½ teaspoon ground black pepper
- ¼ teaspoon red chili flakes
- 1 pound (454 g) Linguine noodles, halved
- Fresh basil leaves for garnish
- ½ cup Parmigiano-Reggiano cheese, grated

1. Warm oil on Sauté. Add onion and Sauté for 2 minutes until soft. Mix garlic and tomatoes and sauté for 4 minutes. To the pot, add vegetable stock, salt, julienned basil, red chili flakes and pepper.
2. Add linguine to the tomato mixture until covered. Seal the lid and cook on High Pressure for 5 minutes.
3. Naturally release the pressure for 5 minutes. Stir the mixture to ensure it is broken down.
4. Divide into plates. Top with basil and Parmigiano-Reggiano cheese and serve.

Super Cheesy Tagliatelle

Prep time: 10 minutes | Cook time: 20 minutes | Serves 6

- ¼ cup goat cheese, chevre
- ¼ cup grated Pecorino cheese
- ½ cup grated Parmesan
- 1 cup heavy cream
- ½ cup grated Gouda
- 2 tablespoons olive oil
- 1 tablespoon Italian seasoning mix
- 1 cup vegetable broth
- 1 pound (454 g) tagliatelle

1. In a bowl, mix goat cheese, pecorino, Parmesan, and heavy cream. Stir in Italian seasoning. Transfer to your instant pot. Stir in the broth and olive oil.
2. Seal the lid and cook on High Pressure for 4 minutes. Do a quick release. Meanwhile, drop the tagliatelle in boiling water and cook for 6 minutes.
3. Remove the instant pot's lid and stir in the tagliatelle. Top with grated gouda and let simmer for about 10 minutes on Sauté mode.

Chickpea Curry

Prep time: 10 minutes | Cook time: 24 minutes | Serves 4

- ½ cup raw chickpeas
- 1½ tablespoons cooking oil
- ½ cup chopped onions
- 1 bay leaf
- ½ tablespoon grated garlic
- ¼ tablespoon grated ginger
- ¾ cup water
- 1 cup fresh tomato purée
- ½ green chili, finely chopped
- ¼ teaspoon turmeric
- ½ teaspoon coriander powder
- 1 teaspoon chili powder
- 1 cup chopped baby spinach
- Salt, to taste
- Boiled white rice, for serving

1. Add the oil and onions to the Instant Pot. Sauté for 5 minutes.
2. Stir in ginger, garlic paste, green chili and bay leaf. Cook for 1 minute, then add all the spices.
3. Add the chickpeas, tomato purée and the water to the pot.
4. Cover and secure the lid. Turn its pressure release handle to the sealing position.
5. Cook on the Manual function with High Pressure for 15 minutes.
6. After the beep, do a Natural release for 20 minutes.
7. Stir in spinach and cook for 3 minutes on the Sauté setting.
8. Serve hot with boiled white rice.

Chicken and Spaghetti Ragù Bolognese

Prep time: 15 minutes | Cook time: 42 minutes | Serves 8

- 2 tablespoons olive oil
- 6 ounces (170 g) bacon, cubed
- 1 onion, minced
- 1 carrot, minced
- 1 celery stalk, minced
- 2 garlic cloves, crushed
- ¼ cup tomato paste
- ¼ teaspoon crushed red pepper

- flakes
- 1½ pounds (680 g) ground chicken
- ½ cup white wine
- 1 cup milk
- 1 cup chicken broth
- Salt, to taste
- 1 pound (454 g) spaghetti

1. Warm oil on Sauté. Add bacon and fry for 5 minutes until crispy.
2. Add celery, carrot, garlic and onion and cook for 5 minutes until fragrant. Mix in red pepper flakes and tomato paste, and cook for 2 minutes. Break chicken into small pieces and place in the pot.
3. Cook for 10 minutes, as you stir, until browned. Pour in wine and simmer for 2 minutes. Add chicken broth and milk. Seal the lid and cook for 15 minutes on High Pressure. Release the pressure quickly.
4. Add the spaghetti and stir. Seal the lid, and cook on High Pressure for another 5 minutes.
5. Release the pressure quickly. Check the pasta for doneness. Taste, adjust the seasoning and serve hot.

Gouda Beef and Spinach Fettuccine

Prep time: 10 minutes | Cook time: 15 minutes | Serves 6

- 10 ounces (283 g) ground beef
- 1 pound (454 g) fettuccine pasta
- 1 cup gouda cheese, shredded
- 1 cup fresh spinach, torn
- 1 medium onion, chopped

- 2 cups tomatoes, diced
- 1 tablespoon olive oil
- 1 teaspoon salt
- ½ teaspoon ground black pepper

1. Heat the olive oil on Sauté mode in the Instant Pot. Stir-fry the beef and onion for 5 minutes. Add the pasta. Pour water enough to cover and season with salt and pepper. Cook on High Pressure for 5 minutes.
2. Do a quick release. Press Sauté and stir in the tomato and spinach; cook for 5 minutes. Top with Gouda to serve.

Chard and Mushroom Risotto

- 3 tablespoons olive oil
- 1 onion, chopped
- 2 Swiss chard, stemmed and chopped
- 1 cup risotto rice
- $1/3$ cup white wine
- 3 cups vegetable stock
- ½ teaspoon salt
- ½ cup mushrooms
- 4 tablespoons pumpkin seeds, toasted
- $1/3$ cup grated Pecorino Romano cheese

1. Heat oil on Sauté, and cook onion and mushrooms for 5 minutes, stirring, until tender. Add the rice and cook for a minute. Stir in wine and cook for 2 to 3 minutes until almost evaporated.
2. Pour in stock and season with salt. Seal the lid and cook on High Pressure for 10 minutes. Do a quick release. Stir in chard until wilted, mix in cheese to melt, and serve scattered with pumpkin seeds.

Red Bean Curry

- ½ cup raw red beans
- 1½ tablespoons cooking oil
- ½ cup chopped onions
- 1 bay leaf
- ½ tablespoon grated garlic
- ¼ tablespoon grated ginger
- ¾ cup water
- 1 cup fresh tomato purée
- ½ green chili, finely chopped
- ¼ teaspoon turmeric
- ½ teaspoon coriander powder
- 1 teaspoon chili powder
- 1 cup chopped baby spinach
- Salt, to taste
- Boiled white rice or quinoa to serve

1. Add the oil and onions to the Instant Pot. Sauté for 5 minutes.
2. Stir in ginger, garlic paste, green chili and bay leaf. Cook for 1 minute, then add all the spices.
3. Add the red beans, tomato purée and water to the pot.
4. Cover and secure the lid. Turn its pressure release handle to the sealing position.
5. Cook on the Manual function with High Pressure for 15 minutes.
6. After the beep, do a Natural release for 20 minutes.
7. Stir in spinach and cook for 3 minutes on the Sauté setting.
8. Serve hot with boiled white rice or quinoa

Asparagus and Broccoli Primavera Farfalle

Prep time: 15 minutes | Cook time: 12 minutes | Serves 4

- 1 bunch asparagus, trimmed, cut into 1-inch pieces
- 2 cups broccoli florets
- 3 tablespoons olive oil
- 3 teaspoons salt
- 10 ounces (283 g) egg noodles
- 3 garlic cloves, minced
- 2½ cups vegetable stock
- ½ cup heavy cream
- 1 cup small tomatoes, halved
- ¼ cup chopped basil
- ½ cup grated Parmesan cheese

1. Pour 2 cups of water, add the noodles, 2 tablespoons of olive oil, garlic and salt. Place a trivet over the water. Combine asparagus, broccoli, remaining olive oil and salt in a bowl. Place the vegetables on the trivet.
2. Seal the lid and cook on Steam for 12 minutes on High. Do a quick release. Remove the vegetables to a plate. Stir the heavy cream and tomatoes in the pasta. Press Sauté and simmer the cream until desired consistency. Gently mix in the asparagus and broccoli. Garnish with basil and Parmesan, to serve.

Turkey and Bell Pepper Tortiglioni

Prep time: 20 minutes | Cook time: 10 minutes | Serves 6

- 2 teaspoons chili powder
- 1 teaspoon salt
- 1 teaspoon cumin
- 1 teaspoon onion powder
- 1 teaspoon garlic powder
- ½ teaspoon thyme
- 1½ pounds (680 g) turkey breast, cut into strips
- 1 tablespoon olive oil
- 1 red onion, cut into wedges
- 4 garlic cloves, minced
- 3 cups chicken broth
- 1 cup salsa
- 1 pound (454 g) tortiglioni
- 1 red bell pepper, chopped diagonally
- 1 yellow bell pepper, chopped diagonally
- 1 green bell pepper, chopped diagonally
- 1 cup shredded Gouda cheese
- ½ cup sour cream
- ½ cup chopped parsley

1. In a bowl, mix chili powder, cumin, garlic powder, onion powder, salt, and oregano. Reserve 1 teaspoon of seasoning. Coat turkey with the remaining seasoning.
2. Warm oil on Sauté. Add turkey strips and sauté for 4 to 5 minutes until browned. Place the turkey in a bowl. Sauté the onion and garlic for 1 minute in the cooker until soft. Press Cancel.

3. Mix in salsa, broth, and scrape the bottom of any brown bits. Into the broth mixture, stir in tortiglioni pasta and cover with bell peppers and chicken.
4. Seal the lid and cook for 5 minutes on High Pressure. Do a quick Pressure release.
5. Open the lid and sprinkle with shredded gouda cheese and reserved seasoning, and stir well. Divide into plates and top with sour cream. Add parsley for garnishing and serve.

Spinach and Ricotta Stuffed Pasta Shells

Prep time: 15 minutes | Cook time: 35 minutes | Serves 6

- 2 cups onion, chopped
- 1 cup carrot, chopped
- 3 garlic cloves, minced
- 3½ tablespoons olive oil,
- 1 (28-ounce / 794-g) canned tomatoes, crushed
- 12 ounces (340 g) conchiglie pasta
- 1 tablespoon olive oil
- 2 cups ricotta cheese, crumbled
- 1½ cup feta cheese, crumbled
- 2 cups spinach, chopped
- ¾ cup grated Pecorino Romano cheese
- 2 tablespoons chopped fresh chives
- 1 tablespoon chopped fresh dill
- Salt and ground black pepper to taste
- 1 cup shredded Cheddar cheese

1. Warm olive oil on Sauté. Add onion, carrot, and garlic, and cook for 5 minutes until tender. Stir in tomatoes and cook for another 10 minutes. Remove to a bowl and set aside.
2. Wipe the pot with a damp cloth, add pasta and cover with enough water. Seal the lid and cook for 5 minutes on High Pressure. Do a quick release and drain the pasta. Lightly Grease olive oil to a baking sheet.
3. In a bowl, combine feta and ricotta cheese. Add spinach, Pecorino Romano cheese, dill, and chives, and stir well. Adjust the seasonings. Using a spoon, fill the shells with the mixture.
4. Spread 4 cups tomato sauce on the baking sheet. Place the stuffed shells over with seam-sides down and sprinkle Cheddar cheese atop. Use aluminum foil to the cover the baking dish.
5. Pour 1 cup of water in the pot of the Pressure cooker and insert the trivet. Lower the baking dish onto the trivet. Seal the lid, and cook for 15 minutes on High Pressure. Do a quick pressure release. Take away the foil. Place the stuffed shells to serving plates and top with tomato sauce before serving.

CHAPTER 5

FISH AND SHELLFISH

Steamed Cod

- 1 pound (454 g) cherry tomatoes, halved
- 1 bunch fresh thyme sprigs
- 4 fillets cod
- 1 teaspoon olive oil
- 1 clove garlic, pressed
- 3 pinches salt
- 2 cups water
- 1 cup white rice
- 1 cup Kalamata olives
- 2 tablespoons pickled capers
- 1 tablespoon olive oil
- 1 pinch ground black pepper

1. Line a parchment paper on the basket of your instant pot. Place about half the tomatoes in a single layer on the paper. Sprinkle with thyme, reserving some for garnish.
2. Arrange cod fillets on top. Sprinkle with a little bit of olive oil.
3. Spread the garlic, pepper, salt, and remaining tomatoes over the fish. In the pot, mix rice and water.
4. Lay a trivet over the rice and water. Lower steamer basket onto the trivet.
5. Seal the lid, and cook for 7 minutes on Low Pressure. Release the pressure quickly.
6. Remove the steamer basket and trivet from the pot. Use a fork to fluff rice.
7. Plate the fish fillets and apply a garnish of olives, reserved thyme, pepper, remaining olive oil, and capers. Serve with rice.

Scallop Teriyaki

- 2 pounds (907 g) jumbo sea scallops
- 2 tablespoons olive oil
- 6 tablespoons pure maple syrup
- 1 cup coconut aminos
- 1 teaspoon ground ginger
- 1 teaspoon garlic powder
- 1 teaspoon sea salt

1. Add the olive oil to the Instant pot and heat it on the Sauté settings of your pot.
2. Add the scallops to the pot and cook for a minute from each side.
3. Stir in all the remaining ingredients in the pot and mix them well.
4. Secure the lid and select the Steam function to cook for 3 minutes.
5. After the beep, do a Quick release then remove the lid.
6. Serve hot.

Steamed Bass

- 1½ cups water
- 1 lemon, sliced
- 4 sea bass fillets
- 4 sprigs thyme
- 1 white onion, cut into thin rings
- 2 turnips, chopped
- 2 pinches salt
- 1 pinch ground black pepper
- 2 teaspoons olive oil

1. Add water and set a rack into the pot.
2. Line a parchment paper to the bottom of the steamer basket. Place lemon slices in a single layer on the rack.
3. Arrange fillets on the top of the lemons, cover with onion and thyme sprigs. Top with turnip slices.
4. Drizzle pepper, salt, and olive oil over the mixture. Put steamer basket onto the rack.
5. Seal lid and cook on Low pressure for 8 minutes. Release the pressure quickly.
6. Serve over the delicate onion rings and thinly turnips.

Rosemary Salmon with Feta Cheese

- 1½ pounds (680 g) salmon fillets
- 1½ cup water
- ¼ cup olive oil
- 1½ garlic clove, minced
- 1½ tablespoon feta cheese, crumbled
- ½ teaspoon dried oregano
- 3 tablespoons fresh lemon juice
- Salt and freshly ground black pepper, to taste
- 3 fresh rosemary sprigs
- 3 lemon slices

1. Take a large bowl and add the garlic, feta cheese, salt, pepper, lemon juice, and oregano. Whisk well all the ingredients.
2. Add the water to the Instant pot then place the steamer trivet in it.
3. Arrange the salmon fillets over the trivet in a single layer.
4. Pour the cheese mixture over these fillets.
5. Place a lemon slice and a rosemary sprig over each fillet.
6. Secure the lid.
7. Select the Steam function on your cooker and set 3 minutes cooking time.
8. After it is done, carefully do a Quick release. Remove the lid.
9. Serve hot.

Catfish and Shrimp Jambalaya

- 4 ounces (113 g) catfish (cut into 1-inch cubes)
- 4 ounces (113 g) shrimp (peeled and deveined)
- 1 tablespoon olive oil
- 2 bacon slices, chopped
- 1¼ cups vegetable broth
- ¾ cup sliced celery stalk
- ¼ teaspoon minced garlic
- ½ cup chopped onion
- 1 cup canned diced tomatoes
- 1 cup uncooked long-grain white rice
- ½ tablespoon Cajun seasoning
- ¼ teaspoon dried thyme
- ¼ teaspoon cayenne pepper
- ½ teaspoon dried oregano
- Salt and freshly ground black pepper, to taste

1. Select the Sauté function on your Instant Pot and add the oil into it.
2. Put the onion, garlic, celery, and bacon to the pot and cook for 10 minutes.
3. Add all the remaining ingredients to the pot except seafood.
4. Stir well, then secure the cooker lid.
5. Select the Slow Cook function on a medium mode.
6. Keep the pressure release handle on venting position. Cook for 4 hours.
7. Once done, remove the lid and add the seafood to the gravy.
8. Secure the lid again, keep the pressure handle in the venting position.
9. Cook for another 45 minutes then serve.

Sardines and Plum Tomato Curry

- 1 tablespoon olive oil
- 1 pound (454 g) fresh sardines, cubed
- 2 plum tomatoes, chopped finely
- ½ large onion, sliced
- 1 garlic clove, minced
- ½ cup tomato purée
- Salt and ground black pepper, to taste

1. Select the Sauté function on your Instant pot then add the oil and sardines to it.
2. Let it sauté for 2 minutes then add all the remaining ingredients.
3. Cover the lid and select Slow Cook function for 8 hours.
4. Remove the lid and stir the cooked curry.
5. Serve warm.

Salmon and Tomato Curry

- 3 pounds (1.4 kg) salmon fillets (cut into pieces)
- 2 tablespoons olive oil
- 2 Serrano peppers, chopped
- 1 teaspoon ground turmeric
- 4 tablespoons curry powder
- 4 teaspoons ground cumin
- 4 curry leaves
- 4 teaspoons ground coriander
- 2 small yellow onions, chopped
- 2 teaspoons red chili powder
- 4 garlic cloves, minced
- 4 cups unsweetened coconut milk
- 2½ cups tomatoes, chopped
- 2 tablespoons fresh lemon juice
- Fresh cilantro leaves to garnish

1. Put the oil and curry leaves to the insert of the Instant Pot. Select the Sauté function to cook for 30 secs.
2. Add the garlic and onions to the pot, cook for 5 minutes.
3. Stir in all the spices and cook for another 1 minute.
4. Put the fish, Serrano pepper, coconut milk, and tomatoes while cooking.
5. Cover and lock the lid. Seal the pressure release valve.
6. Select the Manual function at Low Pressure for 5 minutes.
7. After the beep, do a Natural release to release all the steam.
8. Remove the lid and squeeze in lemon juice.
9. Garnish with fresh cilantro leaves and serve.

Lemony Salmon

- 1 cup water
- 3 lemon slices
- 1 (5-ounce / 142-g) salmon fillet
- 1 teaspoon fresh lemon juice
- Salt and ground black pepper, to taste
- Fresh cilantro to garnish

1. Add the water to the Instant pot and place a trivet inside.
2. In a shallow bowl, place the salmon fillet. Sprinkle salt and pepper over it.
3. Squeeze some lemon juice on top then place a lemon slice over the salmon fillet.
4. Cover the lid and lock it. Set its pressure release handle to Sealing position.
5. Use Steam function on your cooker for 3 minutes to cook.
6. After the beep, do a Quick release and release the pressure.
7. Remove the lid, then serve with the lemon slice and fresh cilantro on top.

Spicy Cumin Salmon

Prep time: 10 minutes | Cook time: 2 minutes | Serves 8

- 2 cups water
- 2 garlic cloves, minced
- 2 teaspoons powdered stevia
- 8 lemon slices
- 2 tablespoons red chili powder
- 2 teaspoons ground cumin
- Salt and freshly grated black pepper, to taste
- 2 pounds (907 g) salmon fillet, cut into 8 pieces

1. Pour two cups of water in the insert of the Instant Pot. Set the trivet in it.
2. In a separate bowl, add all the ingredients except the lemon slices and mix them well.
3. Pour this mixture over the salmon fillets and rub it all over it.
4. Place the salmon slices over the trivet in a single layer.
5. Top each fillet with a lemon slice.
6. Secure the lid and select Steam function for 2 minutes.
7. After the beep, do a Quick release and then remove the lid.
8. Serve immediately.

Shrimps with Broccoli

Prep time: 5 minutes | Cook time: 10 minutes | Serves 2

- 2 teaspoons vegetable oil
- 2 tablespoons corn starch
- 1 cup broccoli florets
- ¼ cup chicken broth
- 8 ounces (227 g) large shrimp, peeled and deveined
- ¼ cup soy sauce
- ¼ cup water
- ¼ cup sliced carrots
- 3 tablespoons rice vinegar
- 2 teaspoons sesame oil
- 1 tablespoon chili garlic sauce
- Coriander leaves to garnish
- Boiled rice or noodles, for serving

1. Add 1 tablespoon of corn starch and shrimp to a bowl. Mix them well then set it aside.
2. In a small bowl, mix the remaining corn starch, chicken broth, carrots, chili garlic sauce, rice vinegar and soy sauce together. Keep the mixture aside.
3. Select the Sauté function on your Instant pot, add the sesame oil and broccoli florets to the pot and sauté for 5 minutes.
4. Add the water to the broccoli, cover the lid and cook for 5 minutes.
5. Stir in shrimp and vegetable oil to the broccoli, sauté it for 5 minutes.
6. Garnish with coriander leaves on top.
7. Serve with rice or noodles.

Rosemary Cod with Cherry Tomato

- 1½ pounds (680 g) cherry tomatoes, halved
- 2½ tablespoons fresh rosemary, chopped
- 6 (4-ounce / 113-g) cod fillets
- 3 garlic cloves, minced
- 2 tablespoons olive oil
- Salt and freshly ground black pepper, to taste

1. Add the olive oil, half of the tomatoes and rosemary to the insert of the Instant Pot.
2. Place the cod fillets over these tomatoes. Then add more tomatoes to the pot.
3. Add the garlic to the pot. Then secure the lid.
4. Select the Manual function with High Pressure for 5 minutes.
5. After the beep, use the quick release to discharge all the steam.
6. Serve cod fillets with tomatoes and sprinkle a pinch of salt and pepper on top.

Mussels with Onions

- 2 tablespoons olive oil
- 2 medium yellow onions, chopped
- 1 teaspoon dried rosemary, crushed
- 2 garlic cloves, minced
- 2 cups chicken broth
- 4 pounds (1.8 kg) mussels, cleaned and debearded
- ¼ cup fresh lemon juice
- Salt and ground black pepper as needed

1. Put the oil to the Instant Pot and select the Sauté function for cooking.
2. Add the onions and cook for 5 minutes with occasional stirring.
3. Add the rosemary and garlic to the pot. Stir and cook for 1 minute.
4. Pour the chicken broth and lemon juice into the cooker, sprinkle some salt and black pepper over it.
5. Place the trivet inside the cooker and arrange the mussels over it.
6. Select the Manual function at Low Pressure for 1 minute.
7. Secure the lid and let the mussels cook.
8. After the beep, do a Quick release then remove the lid.
9. Serve the mussels with its steaming hot soup in a bowl.

Coconut Tangy Cod curry

Prep time: 5 minutes | Cook time: 3 minutes | Serves 6

- 1 (28-ounce / 794-g) can coconut milk
- Juice of 2 lemons
- 2 tablespoons red curry paste
- 2 teaspoons fish sauce
- 2 teaspoons honey
- 4 teaspoons Sriracha
- 4 cloves garlic, minced
- 2 teaspoons ground turmeric
- 2 teaspoons ground ginger
- 1 teaspoon sea salt
- 1 teaspoon white pepper
- 2 pounds (907 g) codfish, cut into 1-inch cubes
- ½ cup chopped fresh cilantro, for garnish
- 4 lime wedges, for garnish

1. Add all the ingredients, except the cod cubes and garnish, to a large bowl and whisk them well.
2. Arrange the cod cube at the base of the Instant Pot and pour the coconut milk mixture over it.
3. Secure the lid and hit the Manual key, select High Pressure with 3 minutes cooking time.
4. After the beep, do a Quick release then remove the lid.
5. Garnish with fresh cilantro and lemon wedges then serve.

Mahi-Mahi and Tomato Bowls

Prep time: 5 minutes | Cook time: 14 minutes | Serves 3

- 3 (4-ounce / 113-g) mahi-mahi fillets
- 1½ tablespoons olive oil
- ½ yellow onion, sliced
- ½ teaspoon dried oregano
- 1 tablespoon fresh lemon juice
- Salt and freshly ground black pepper, to taste
- 1 (14-ounce / 397-g) can sugar-free diced tomatoes

1. Add the olive oil to the Instant Pot. Select the Sauté function on it.
2. Add all the ingredient to the pot except the fillets. Cook them for 10 minutes.
3. Press the Cancel key, then add the mahi-mahi fillets to the sauce.
4. Cover the fillets with sauce by using a spoon.
5. Secure the lid and set the Manual function at High Pressure for 4 minutes.
6. After the beep, do a Quick release then remove the lid.
7. Serve the fillets with their sauce, poured on top.

Cod Curry

- 3 pounds (1.4 kg) cod fillets, cut into bite-sized pieces
- 2 tablespoons olive oil
- 4 curry leaves
- 4 medium onions, chopped
- 2 tablespoons fresh ginger, grated finely
- 4 garlic cloves, minced
- 4 tablespoons curry powder
- 4 teaspoons ground cumin
- 4 teaspoons ground coriander
- 2 teaspoons red chili powder
- 1 teaspoon ground turmeric
- 4 cups unsweetened coconut milk
- 2½ cups tomatoes, chopped
- 2 Serrano peppers, seeded and chopped
- 2 tablespoons fresh lemon juice

1. Add the oil to the Instant Pot and select Sauté function for cooking.
2. Add the curry leaves and cook for 30 seconds. Stir the onion, garlic, and ginger into the pot and cook 5 minutes.
3. Add all the spices to the mixture and cook for another 1½ minutes.
4. Hit Cancel then add the coconut milk, Serrano pepper, tomatoes, and fish to the pot.
5. Secure the lid and select the Manual settings with Low Pressure and 5 minutes cooking time.
6. After the beep, do a Quick release and remove the lid.
7. Drizzle lemon juice over the curry then stir.
8. Serve immediately.

Tuna with Shirataki Noodles

- ½ can tuna, drained
- 8 ounces (227 g) Shirataki noodles
- ½ cup frozen peas
- 1 (14-ounce / 397-g) can cream
- mushroom soup
- 2 ounces (57 g) shredded Cheddar cheese
- 1½ cups water

1. Add the water with noodles to the base of your Instant Pot.
2. Place the tuna and peas over it. Then pour the mushroom soup on top.
3. Secure the lid and cook with the Manual function at High Pressure for 4 minutes.
4. After the beep, do a Quick release then remove the lid.
5. Stir in shredded cheese to the tuna mix.
6. Serve warm.

Alfredo Tuscan Shrimp with Penne

Prep time: 5 minutes | Cook time: 5 minutes | Serves 3

- 1 pound (454 g) shrimp
- 1 jar alfredo sauce
- 1½ cups fresh spinach
- 1 cup sun-dried tomatoes
- 1 box penne pasta
- 1½ teaspoon Tuscan seasoning
- 3 cups water

1. Add the water and pasta to a pot over a medium heat, boil until it cooks completely. Then strain the pasta and keep it aside.
2. Select the Sauté function on your Instant Pot and add the tomatoes, shrimp, Tuscan seasoning, and alfredo sauce into it.
3. Stir and cook until shrimp turn pink in color.
4. Now add the spinach leaves to the pot and cook for 5 minutes.
5. Add the pasta to the pot and stir well.
6. Serve hot.

Grits with Shrimp

Prep time: 5 minutes | Cook time: 15 minutes | Serves 8

- 1 tablespoon olive oil
- 2 cups quick grits
- 12 ounces (340 g) Parmesan cheese, shredded
- 2 cups heavy cream
- 24 ounces (680 g) tail-on shrimp
- 2 tablespoons Old Bay seasoning
- A pinch of ground black pepper
- 4 cups water

1. Add the olive oil to the Instant Pot. Select the Sauté function for cooking.
2. Add the shrimp to the oil and drizzle old bay seasoning over it.
3. Cook the shrimp for 3 to 4 minutes while stirring then set them aside.
4. Now add the water, cream, and quick grits to the pot. Select the Manual function for 3 minutes at High Pressure.
5. After the beep, do a quick pressure release then remove the lid.
6. Add the shredded cheese to the grits then stir well.
7. Take a serving bowl, first pour in the creamy grits mixture then top it with shrimp.
8. Sprinkle black pepper on top then serve hot.

Shrimps with Northern Beans

Prep time: 10 minutes | Cook time: 25 minutes | Serves 3

- 1½ tablespoons olive oil
- 1 medium onion, chopped
- ½ small green bell pepper, seeded and chopped
- ½ celery stalk, chopped
- 1 garlic clove, minced
- 1 tablespoon fresh parsley, chopped
- ½ teaspoon red pepper flakes, crushed
- ½ teaspoon cayenne pepper
- ½ pound (227 g) great northern beans, rinsed, soaked, and drained
- 1 cup chicken broth
- 1 bay leaf
- ½ pound (227 g) medium shrimp, peeled and deveined

1. Select the Sauté function on your Instant pot, then add the oil, onion, celery, bell pepper and cook for 5 minutes.
2. Now add the parsley, garlic, spices, and bay leaf to the pot and cook for another 2 minutes.
3. Pour in the chicken broth then add the beans to it. Secure the cooker lid.
4. Select the Manual function for 15 minutes with medium pressure.
5. After the beep, do a Natural release for 10 minutes and remove the lid.
6. Add the shrimp to the beans and cook them together on the Manual function for 2 minutes at High Pressure.
7. Do a Quick release, keep it aside for 10 minutes, then remove the lid.
8. Serve hot.

Shrimp and Tomato Creole

Prep time: 20 minutes | Cook time: 7 hours 10 minutes | Serves 4

- 1 pound (454 g) shrimp (peeled and deveined)
- 1 tablespoon olive oil
- 1 (28-ounce / 794-g) can crush whole tomatoes
- 1 cup celery stalk (sliced)
- ¾ cup chopped white onion
- ½ cup green bell pepper (chopped)
- 1 (8-ounce / 227-g) can tomato sauce
- ½ teaspoon minced garlic
- ¼ teaspoon ground black pepper
- 1 tablespoon Worcestershire sauce
- 4 drops hot pepper sauce
- Salt, to taste
- White rice for serving

1. Put the oil to the Instant Pot along with all the ingredients except the shrimp.
2. Secure the cooker lid and keep the pressure handle valve turned to the venting position.

3. Select the Slow Cook function on your cooker and set it on medium heat.
4. Let the mixture cook for 6 hours.
5. Remove the lid afterwards and add the shrimp to the pot.
6. Stir and let the shrimp cook for another 1 hour on Slow Cook function.
7. Keep the lid covered with pressure release handle in the venting position.
8. To serve, pour the juicy shrimp creole over steaming white rice.

Teriyaki Salmon

Prep time: 10 minutes | Cook time: 8 minutes | Serves 4

- 4 (8-ounce / 227-g) thick salmon fillets.
- 1 cup soy sauce
- 2 cups water
- ½ cup mirin
- 2 tablespoons sesame oil
- 4 teaspoons sesame seeds
- 2 cloves garlic, minced
- 2 tablespoons freshly grated ginger
- 4 tablespoons brown sugar
- 1 tablespoon corn starch
- 4 green onions, minced

1. Add the soy sauce, sesame oil, sesame seeds, mirin, ginger, water, garlic, green onions, and brown sugar to a small bowl. Mix them well.
2. In a shallow dish place the salmon fillets and pour half of the prepared mixture over the fillets. Let it marinate for 30 minutes in a refrigerator.
3. Pour 1 cup of water into the insert of your Instant pot and place trivet inside it.
4. Arrange the marinated salmon fillets over the trivet and secure the lid.
5. Select the Manual settings with High Pressure and 8 minutes cooking time.
6. Meanwhile, take a skillet and add the remaining marinade mixture in it.
7. Let it cook for 2 minutes, then add the corn starch mixed with water. Stir well and cook for 1 minute.
8. Check the pressure cooker, do a Quick release if it is done.
9. Transfer the fillets to a serving platter and pour the sesame mixture over it.
10. Garnish with chopped green chilies then serve hot.

Salmon and Potato Casserole

Prep time: 20 minutes | Cook time: 8 hours | Serves 4

- ½ tablespoon olive oil
- 8 ounces (227 g) cream of mushroom soup
- ¼ cup water
- 3 medium potatoes (peeled and sliced)
- 3 tablespoons flour

- 1 (1-pound / 454-g) can salmon (drained and flaked)
- ½ cup chopped scallion
- ¼ teaspoon ground nutmeg
- Salt and freshly ground black pepper, to taste

1. Pour mushroom soup and water in a separate bowl and mix them well.
2. Add the olive oil to the Instant Pot and grease it lightly.
3. Place half of the potatoes in the pot and sprinkle salt, pepper, and half of the flour over it.
4. Now add a layer of half of the salmon over potatoes, then a layer of half of the scallions.
5. Repeat these layers and pour mushroom soup mix on top.
6. Top it with nutmeg evenly.
7. Secure the lid and set its pressure release handle to the venting position.
8. Select the Slow Cook function with Medium heat on your Instant Pot.
9. Let it cook for 8 hours then serve.

Shrimp and Potato Curry

Prep time: 5 minutes | Cook time: 9 minutes | Serves 8

- 2 tablespoons olive oil
- 1½ medium onion, chopped
- 1½ teaspoons ground cumin
- 2 teaspoons red chili powder
- 2 teaspoons ground turmeric
- 3 medium white rose potatoes, diced

- 6 medium tomatoes, chopped
- 2 pounds (907 g) medium shrimp, peeled and deveined
- 1½ tablespoons fresh lemon juice
- Salt, to taste
- ½ cup fresh cilantro, chopped

1. Select the Sauté function on your Instant Pot. Add the oil and onions then cook for 2 minutes.
2. Add the tomatoes, potatoes, cilantro, lemon juice and all the spices into the pot and secure the lid.
3. Select the Manual function at medium pressure for 5 minutes.

4. Do a natural release then remove the lid. Stir shrimp into the pot.
5. Secure the lid again then set the Manual function with High Pressure for 2 minutes.
6. After the beep, use Natural release and let it stand for 10 minutes.
7. Remove the lid and serve hot.

Shrimp and Spaghetti Squash Bowls

- ½ cup dry white wine
- ¼ teaspoon crushed red pepper flakes
- 1 large shallot, finely chopped
- 1 pound (454 g) jumbo shrimp, peeled and deveined
- 1 (28-ounce / 794-g) can crushed
- tomatoes
- 2 cloves garlic, minced
- 2½ pounds (1.1 kg) spaghetti squash
- 1 teaspoon olive oil
- Salt and pepper, to taste
- Parsley leaves (garnish)

1. At first, sprinkle some salt and pepper over the shrimp and keep them in a refrigerator until further use.
2. Hit the Sauté function on your Instant Pot, then add the olive oil and red pepper flakes into it. Sauté for 1 minute.
3. Add the shallot and cook for 3 minutes. Then add the garlic, cook for 1 minute.
4. Add the dry wine, tomatoes, and whole spaghetti squash in the pot. Select Manual settings with medium pressure for 20 minutes.
5. After the beep, do a Natural release. Remove the lid and the spaghetti squash.
6. Cut squash in half, remove its seed and stab with a fork to form spaghetti strands out of it. Keep them aside.
7. Select the Sauté function on your instant pot again, stir in shrimp.
8. Mix well the shrimp with sauce.
9. To serve, top the spaghetti squash with shrimp and sauce. Garnish it with parsley.

CHAPTER
6

CHICKEN, BEEF, PORK, AND LAMB

Chicken Legs with Capers and Pickles

Prep time: 10 minutes | Cook time: 22 minutes | Serves 4

- 4 chicken legs
- Sea salt and black pepper, to taste
- 2 tablespoons olive oil
- 1 onion, diced
- 2 garlic cloves, minced
- $1/_3$ cup red wine
- 2 cups diced tomatoes
- $1/_3$ cup capers
- ¼ cup fresh basil
- 2 pickles, chopped

1. Sprinkle pepper and salt over the chicken. Warm oil on Sauté. Add onion and Sauté for 3 minutes until fragrant. Add garlic and cook for 30 seconds until softened.
2. Mix the chicken with vegetables and cook for 6 to 7 minutes until lightly browned.
3. Add red wine to the pan to deglaze, scrape the pan's bottom to get rid of any browned bits of food; Stir in tomatoes. Seal the lid and cook on High Pressure for 12 minutes. Release the pressure quickly.
4. To the chicken mixture, add basil, capers and pickles. Serve the chicken topped with the tomato sauce mixture.

Beef Gyros

Prep time: 15 minutes | Cook time: 30 minutes | Serves 4

- 1 pound (454 g) beef sirloin, cut into thin strips
- 1 onion, thinly chopped
- $1/_3$ cup beef broth
- 2 tablespoons fresh lemon juice
- 2 tablespoons olive oil
- 2 teaspoons dry oregano
- 1 clove garlic, minced
- Salt and ground black pepper to taste
- 4 slices pita bread
- 1 cup Greek yogurt
- 2 tablespoons fresh dill, chopped

1. In the pot, mix beef, beef broth, oregano, garlic, lemon juice, pepper, onion, olive oil, and salt.
2. Seal the lid and cook on High Pressure for 30 minutes. Release pressure naturally for 15 minutes, then turn steam vent valve to Venting to release the remaining Pressure quickly.
3. Divide the beef mixture between the pita breads, Top with yogurt and dill, and roll up to serve.

Herbed Whole Chicken

Prep time: 15 minutes | Cook time: 36 minutes | Serves 6

- 1 cup chicken stock
- ½ cup white wine
- ½ onion, thinly chopped
- 2 cloves garlic, minced
- 1 (3½-pound / 1.6-kg) whole chicken, patted dry with paper
- towel
- 1 teaspoon salt
- ½ teaspoon ground black pepper
- ½ teaspoon dried thyme
- 2 tablespoons olive oil
- ½ teaspoon paprika

1. Into the pot, add onion, chicken stock, white wine, and garlic. Over the mixture, place a steamer rack.
2. Rub pepper, salt, and thyme onto chicken; lay onto the rack breast-side up. Seal the lid, press Poultry and cook on High Pressure for 26 minutes. Release the pressure quickly.
3. While pressure releases, preheat oven broiler. In a bowl, mix paprika and olive oil. Remove the rack with chicken from your pot. Get rid of onion and stock. Onto the chicken, brush the mixture and take the rack back to the pot. Cook under the broiler for 5 minutes until chicken skin is crispy and browned.
4. Set chicken to a cutting board to cool for about 5 minutes, then carve and transfer to a serving platter.

Pork and Mushroom Estofado

Prep time: 15 minutes | Cook time: 35 minutes | Serves 4

- 12 ounces (340 g) pork neck, cut into bite-sized pieces
- 2 tablespoons flour
- 1 tablespoon fennel seeds, crushed
- 4 tablespoons vegetable oil
- 2 onions, peeled, chopped
- 1 carrot
- A handful of chopped celery
- 10 ounces (283 g) button mushrooms
- 4 cups beef broth
- 1 chili pepper, chopped
- 1 tablespoon cayenne pepper

1. Heat oil on Sauté. Add onions and cook for 2 minutes, until translucent. Add flour, chili pepper, carrot, celery, cayenne pepper, and fennel seeds, and continue cooking for 2 more minutes, stirring constantly.
2. Press Cancel, and add meat, mushrooms, beef broth, and water. Seal the lid and cook on Manual/Pressure Cook mode for 30 minutes on High Pressure. Do a quick release and serve immediately.

Salsa Chicken

Prep time: 5 minutes | Cook time: 25 minutes | Serves 6

- 2 pounds (907 g) boneless skinless chicken drumsticks
- ¼ teaspoon salt
- 1½ cups hot tomato salsa
- 1 onion, chopped
- 1 cup feta cheese, crumbled

1. Sprinkle salt over the chicken; and set in the instant pot. Stir in salsa to coat the chicken. Seal the lid and cook for 15 minutes on High Pressure. Do a quick Pressure release. Press Sauté and cook for 5-10 minutes as you stir until excess liquid has evaporated. Top with feta cheese to serve.

Tangy Chicken and Asparagus Bowls

Prep time: 15 minutes | Cook time: 25 minutes | Serves 4

- 1 (3½-pound / 1.6-kg) Young Whole Chicken
- 4 garlic cloves, minced
- 1 teaspoon olive oil
- 4 fresh thyme, minced
- 3 fresh rosemary, minced
- 2 lemons, zested and quartered
- Salt and freshly ground black pepper to taste
- 2 tablespoons olive oil
- 8 ounces (227 g) asparagus, trimmed and chopped
- 1 onion, chopped
- 1 cup chicken stock
- 1 tablespoon soy sauce
- 1 fresh thyme sprig
- Cooking spray
- 1 tablespoon flour
- Chopped parsley to garnish

1. Rub all sides of the chicken with garlic, rosemary, black pepper, lemon zest, thyme, and salt. Into the chicken cavity, insert lemon wedges. Warm oil on Sauté. Add onion and asparagus, and sauté for 5 minutes until softened. Mix chicken stock, 1 thyme sprig, black pepper, soy sauce, and salt.
2. Into the inner pot, set trivet over asparagus mixture. On top of the trivet, place the chicken with breast-side up.
3. Seal the lid, select Poultry and cook for 20 minutes on High Pressure. Do a quick release. Remove the chicken to a serving platter.
4. In the inner pot, sprinkle flour over asparagus mixture and blend the sauce with an immersion blender until desired consistency. Top the chicken with asparagus sauce and garnish with parsley.

Chicken with Potatoes

- 4 potatoes, peeled and quartered
- 4 cups water
- 2 lemons, zested and juiced
- 1 tablespoon olive oil
- 2 teaspoons fresh oregano
- Salt, to taste
- ¼ teaspoon freshly ground black pepper
- 2 Serrano peppers, stemmed, cored, and chopped
- 4 boneless skinless chicken drumsticks
- 3 tablespoons finely chopped parsley
- 1 cup packed watercress
- 1 cucumber, thinly chopped
- ½ cup cherry tomatoes, quartered
- ¼ cup Kalamata olives, pitted
- ¼ cup hummus
- ¼ cup feta cheese, crumbled
- Lemon wedges, for serving

1. In the cooker, add water and potatoes. Set trivet over them. In a baking bowl, mix lemon juice, olive oil, black pepper, oregano, zest, salt, and red pepper flakes. Add chicken drumsticks in the marinade and stir to coat.
2. Set the bowl with chicken on the trivet in the inner pot. Seal the lid, select Poultry and cook on High for 15 minutes. Do a quick release. Take out the bowl with chicken and the trivet from the pot. Drain potatoes and add parsley and salt.
3. Split the potatoes among four serving plates and top with watercress, cucumber slices, hummus, cherry tomatoes, chicken, olives, and feta cheese. Each bowl should be garnished with a lemon wedge.

Chicken and Black Olive Cacciatore

- 2 teaspoons olive oil
- 1 pound (454 g) chicken drumsticks, boneless, skinless
- 2 teaspoons salt
- 1½ teaspoons freshly ground black pepper
- 1carrot, chopped
- 1 red bell pepper, chopped
- 1 yellow bell pepper, chopped
- 1 onion, chopped
- 4 garlic cloves, minced
- 2 teaspoons dried oregano
- 1 teaspoon dried basil
- 1 teaspoon dried parsley
- 1 pinch red pepper flakes
- 1 (28-ounce / 794-g) can diced tomatoes
- ½ cup dry red wine
- ¾ cup chicken stock
- 1 cup black olives, pitted and chopped
- 2 bay leaves

1. Warm oil on Sauté mode. Season the drumsticks with pepper and salt. In batches, sear the chicken for 5-6 minutes until golden-brown. Set aside on a plate. Drain the pot and remain with 1 tablespoon of fat.
2. In the hot oil, Sauté onion, garlic, and bell peppers for 4 minutes until softened; add red pepper flakes, basil, parsley, and oregano, and cook for 30 more seconds. Season with salt and pepper.
3. Stir in tomatoes, olives, chicken stock, red wine and bay leaves.
4. Return chicken to the pot. Seal the lid and cook on High Pressure for 15 minutes. Release the pressure quickly. Divide chicken into four serving bowls; Top with tomato mixture before serving.

Chicken and Veg Bowls

Prep time: 15 minutes | Cook time: 20 minutes | Serves 4

- 4 skin-on, bone-in chicken legs
- 2 tablespoons olive oil
- Salt and freshly ground black pepper to taste
- 4 cloves garlic, minced
- 1 teaspoon fresh chopped thyme
- ½ cup dry white wine
- 1¼ cups chicken stock
- 1 cup carrots, thinly chopped
- 1 cup parsnip, thinly chopped
- 3 tomatoes, thinly chopped
- 1 tablespoon honey
- 4 slices lemon
- Fresh thyme, chopped for garnish

1. Season the chicken with pepper and salt. Warm oil on Sauté mode.
2. Arrange chicken legs into the hot oil; cook for 3 to 5 minutes each side until browned. Place in a bowl and set aside. Sauté thyme and garlic in the chicken fat for 1 minute until soft and lightly golden.
3. Add wine into the pot to deglaze, scrape the pot's bottom to get rid of any brown bits of food. Simmer the wine for 2 to 3 minutes until slightly reduced in volume.
4. Add stock, carrots, parsnips, tomatoes, pepper and salt into the pot. Lay steam rack onto veggies.
5. Into the pressure cooker's steamer basket, arrange chicken legs. Set the steamer basket onto the rack.
6. Drizzle the chicken with honey then Top with lemon slices.
7. Seal the lid and cook on High Pressure for 12 minutes. Release pressure naturally for 10 minutes.
8. Place the chicken to a bowl. Drain the veggies and place them around the chicken. Garnish with fresh thyme leaves before serving.

Chicken and Bean Lettuce Wraps

- 2 tablespoons canola oil
- 2 pounds (907 g) chicken thighs, boneless, skinless
- 1 cup pineapple juice
- 1/3 cup water
- ¼ cup soy sauce
- 2 tablespoons maple syrup
- 1 tablespoon rice vinegar
- 1 teaspoon chili-garlic sauce
- 3 tablespoons cornstarch
- Salt and freshly ground black pepper to taste
- 12 large lettuce leaves
- 2 cups canned pinto beans, rinsed and drained

1. Warm oil on Sauté. In batches, sear chicken in the oil for 5 minutes until browned. Set aside in a bowl.
2. Into your pot, mix chili-garlic sauce, pineapple juice, soy sauce, vinegar, maple syrup, and water; Stir in chicken to coat. Seal the lid and cook on High Pressure for 7 minutes. Release pressure naturally for 10 minutes. Shred the chicken with two forks. Take ¼ cup liquid from the pot to a bowl; Stir in cornstarch to dissolve.
3. Mix the cornstarch mixture with the mixture in the pot and return the chicken.
4. Select Sauté and cook for 5 minutes until the sauce thickens; add pepper and salt for seasoning.
5. Transfer beans into lettuce leaves, top with chicken carnitas and serve.

Minty Calf's Liver

- 1 pound (454 g) calf's liver, rinsed
- 3 tablespoons olive oil
- 2 garlic cloves, crushed
- 1 tablespoon fresh mint, finely
- chopped
- ½ tablespoon cayenne pepper
- 1 teaspoon salt
- ½ teaspoon Italian Seasoning

1. In a bowl, mix oil, garlic, mint, cayenne, salt and Italian seasoning. Brush the liver and chill for 30 minutes. Remove from the fridge and pat dry with paper.
2. Place the liver into the inner pot. Seal the lid and cook on High Pressure for 5 minutes. When ready, release the pressure naturally, for about 10 minutes.

Pork Schnitzel

- 2 pounds (907 g) boneless pork chops, thinly sliced
- 2 teaspoons water
- 2 eggs
- 4 tablespoons oil
- ¼ cup Parmesan cheese, grated
- ½ teaspoon garlic powder
- 1 teaspoon salt
- 1 teaspoon black pepper
- ½ cup coconut flour
- 1 cup panko breadcrumbs

1. Crack the eggs into a bowl and whisk them together with the water.
2. Stir in the coconut flour, salt, cheese, pepper and garlic powder.
3. Heat the oil using the Sauté function on the instant pot.
4. Take the pork chops, dip them into the egg mixture, then dredge them through the breadcrumbs.
5. Place the chops in the pot and secure the lid.
6. Cook for 10 minutes on Manual setting at High Pressure.
7. Release the steam, open the lid and flip the pork chops over. Secure the lid again.
8. Cook for another 10 minutes at the same settings
9. Release the pressure, remove the lid and serve.

Lamb Leg with Pancetta

- 2 pounds (907 g) lamb leg
- 6 garlic cloves
- 1 large onion, chopped
- 6 pancetta slices
- 1 teaspoon rosemary
- ½ teaspoon salt
- ¼ teaspoon freshly ground black pepper
- 2 tablespoons olive oil
- 3 cups beef broth

1. Heat oil on Sauté. Add pancetta and onions, making two layers. Season with salt and cook for 3 minutes, until browned. Meanwhile, place the meat in a separate dish.
2. Using a sharp knife, make 6 incisions into the meat and place a garlic clove in each. Rub the meat with spices and transfer to the pot. Press Cancel and pour in beef broth. Seal the lid and cook on High pressure for 25 minutes. When done, do a natural pressure release, for about 10 minutes.

Pork and Carrot Bo Kho

- 1¼ pounds (567 g) pork briskets
- 1 tablespoon olive oil
- ½ small onion, diced
- 1 tablespoon fresh ginger, grated
- 1 tablespoon red boat fish sauce
- ½ large stalk lemongrass, cut into 3-inch lengths
- ½ bay leaf
- ½ cup diced tomatoes
- ½ pound (227 g) carrots, peeled and chopped
- 1 teaspoon Madras curry powder
- 1 tablespoon apple sauce
- 1 whole star anise
- ½ cup bone broth
- ½ teaspoon salt

1. Select Sauté function on the instant pot and add the olive oil to it.
2. Stir-fry the briskets in the pot in batches.
3. Transfer the briskets to a plate and put the onions into the pot.
4. Sauté the onions for 3 minutes then add the ginger, carrots, diced tomatoes, curry powder, red boat fish sauce, and the seared pork.
5. Stir in the lemongrass, bay leaf, broth, apple sauce and star anise.
6. Cook on the Manual function for 35 minutes at High Pressure.
7. Release the pressure naturally for 30 minutes then remove the lid.
8. Serve immediately.

Pork and Calabacita Squash Bowls

- ½ pork tenderloin
- ½ tablespoon ground cumin
- 1 teaspoon salt
- ½ tablespoon chili powder
- ½ tablespoon garlic powder
- ½ tablespoon olive oil
- 4 cups water
- 3 calabacita squashes, seeds removed

1. Season the pork with half the cumin, garlic powder, salt and chili powder.
2. Switch the instant pot to Sauté mode and add the olive oil to heat.
3. Place the seasoned pork in the pot and cook it for 4 minutes per side.
4. Pour in 4 cups of water and secure the lid.
5. Select Meat/Stew option and cook for 1 hour.
6. Natural release the pressure for 30 minutes, and remove the lid.
7. Stuff the calabacita squashes with the pork mixture.
8. Serve hot.

Lamb with Rice and Peas

Prep time: 10 minutes | Cook time: 21 minutes | Serves 4

- 1 cup rice
- 1 cup green peas
- 12 ounces (340 g) lamb, tender cuts, ½-inch thick
- 3 tablespoons sesame seeds
- 4 cups beef broth
- 1 teaspoon sea salt
- 1 bay leaf
- ½ teaspoon dried thyme
- 3 tablespoons olive oil

1. Place the meat in the pot and pour in broth. Seal the lid and cook on High Pressure for 13 minutes. Do a quick release. Remove the meat but keep the liquid. Add rice and green peas.
2. Season with salt, bay leaf, and thyme. Stir well and top with the meat. Seal the lid and cook on Rice for 8 minutes on High. Do a quick release and stir in olive oil and sesame seeds. Serve immediately.

Glazed Lamb Chops with Carrots

Prep time: 5 minutes | Cook time: 26 minutes | Serves 2

- 1 pound (454 g) lamb loin chops
- 1 garlic clove, crushed
- ½ cup bone broth
- ¾ teaspoon dried rosemary, crushed
- 1 tablespoon arrowroot starch
- 1½ tablespoons olive oil
- ½ small onion, sliced
- ¾ cup sugar-free, diced tomatoes
- 1 cup carrots, peeled and sliced
- Salt and black pepper, to taste
- ½ tablespoon cold water

1. Add the olive oil to the instant pot and heat it on the Sauté function.
2. Place the lamb chops in the pot and cook for 3 minutes each side.
3. Take the chops out of the pot and place them on a plate.
4. Put the onion and garlic into the pot and cook for 3 minutes.
5. Add the remaining ingredients except the arrowroot and water and secure the lid.
6. Cook on the Manual setting for 15 minutes at High Pressure.
7. Once done Quick release the pressure and remove the lid.
8. Meanwhile, dissolve the arrowroot flour in some water and add the slurry to the pot.
9. Cook for 5 minutes then pour this sauce over the fried chops.
10. Serve hot.

Cauliflower Pork Tourtiere

Prep time: 5 minutes | Cook time: 50 minutes | Serves 10

- 2 (9 inch) pie crust, frozen, ready-to-bake
- 2 pounds (907 g) pork meat
- 1 cup water
- ½ teaspoon black pepper
- 2 teaspoons salt
- ½ teaspoon ground nutmeg
- 1 tablespoon ground sage
- 4 tablespoons olive oil
- 2 small onions, sliced
- 2 cups cooked cauliflower

1. Put the meat, onions, salt and water into the instant pot.
2. Secure the lid and cook for 20 minutes at High Pressure using the Meat/Stew option.
3. Natural release the pressure for 5 minutes, then remove the lid.
4. In a blender, blend the cooked cauliflower and add this mixture to the pot.
5. Stir in the olive oil and all the spices.
6. Mix well and pour the mixture over the pie crust.
7. Bake the pie for 30 minutes at 350ºF (180ºC) in an oven.
8. Serve warm.

Lamb with Bell Peppers

Prep time: 10 minutes | Cook time: 30 minutes | Serves 10

- 2 pounds (907 g) grass-fed, boneless lamb, trimmed
- 4 cups tomatoes, chopped finely
- 6 garlic cloves, minced
- 2 cups water
- 2 tablespoons olive oil
- Salt and black pepper to taste
- 2 teaspoons dried rosemary, crushed
- 2 large green bell peppers, seeded and sliced
- 2 large yellow bell peppers, seeded and sliced
- 2 large red bell peppers, seeded and sliced
- 3 cups sugar-free tomato sauce

1. Turn the instant pot to the Sauté function and add the oil to it.
2. Stir in the lamb meat along with salt and pepper. Cook for 5 minutes.
3. Dish the meat out onto a plate.
4. Add the water, salt, garlic, tomatoes, rosemary and black pepper.
5. Stir in all the peppers, tomato sauce and return the meat to the pot.
6. Secure the lid and set it to the Manual function for 25 minutes at High Pressure.
7. Quick release the pressure and remove the lid. Serve hot.

Lamb Ragout

- 1 pound (454 g) lamb chops, 1-inch thick
- 1 cup water
- 1 cup green peas, rinsed
- 3 carrots, peeled, chopped
- 3 onions, peeled, chopped
- 1 potato, peeled, chopped
- 1 tomato, peeled, roughly chopped
- 3 tablespoons olive oil
- 1 tablespoon paprika
- Salt and black pepper to taste

1. Grease the instant pot with olive oil. Rub salt onto meat and make a bottom layer. Add peas, carrots, onions, potatoes, and tomato. Season with paprika.
2. Add olive oil, water, salt, and pepper. Give it a good stir and seal the lid. Cook on Meat/Stew mode for 20 minutes on High Pressure. When ready, do a natural Pressure release, for about 10 minutes.

Beef Brisket and Bean Carne Asada

- 1 tablespoon ground black pepper
- 2 teaspoons salt
- 1 teaspoon sweet paprika
- 1 teaspoon cayenne pepper
- 1 teaspoon chili powder
- ½ teaspoon garlic salt
- ½ teaspoon onion powder
- 1 (4-pound / 1.8-kg) beef brisket
- 1 cup beef broth
- 2 bay leaves
- 2 tablespoons Worcestershire sauce
- 14 ounces (397 g) canned black beans, drained and rinsed

1. In a bowl, combine pepper, paprika, chili powder, cayenne pepper, salt, onion powder and garlic salt; rub onto brisket pieces to coat.
2. Add the brisket to your instant pot. Cover with Worcestershire sauce and water.
3. Seal the lid and cook on High Pressure for 50 minutes. Release the pressure naturally for 10 minutes.
4. Transfer the brisket to a cutting board. Drain any liquid present in the pot using a fine-mesh strainer; get rid of any solids and fat.
5. Slice brisket, arrange the slices onto a platter, add the black beans on side and spoon the cooking liquid over the slices and beans to serve.

Pork with Squash and Mushroom Sauce

- 3 tablespoons olive oil
- 2 sprigs thyme, leaves removed and chopped
- 2 sprigs rosemary, leaves removed and chopped
- 4 pork chops
- 1 cup mushrooms, chopped
- 4 cloves garlic, minced
- 1 cup chicken broth
- 1 tablespoon soy sauce
- 1 pound (454 g) butternut squash, cubed
- 1 tablespoon olive oil
- 1 teaspoon cornstarch

1. Set on Sauté and heat rosemary, thyme and 2 tablespoons of oil. Add the pork chops and sear for 1 minute for each side until lightly browned.
2. Sauté garlic and mushrooms in the instant pot for 5-6 minutes until mushrooms are tender. Add soy sauce and broth. Transfer pork chops to a wire trivet and place it into the pot. Over the chops, place a cake pan. Add butternut squash in the pot and drizzle with 1 tablespoon olive oil.
3. Seal the lid and cook on High Pressure for 10 minutes. Release the pressure quickly. Remove the pan and trivet from the pot. Stir cornstarch into the mushroom mixture for 2 to 3 minutes until the sauce thickens.
4. Transfer the mushroom sauce to an immersion blender and blend until you attain the desired consistency. Scoop sauce into a cup with a pour spout. Smash the squash into a purée. Set pork chops on a plate and ladle squash purée next to them. Top the pork chops with gravy.

Orange Pork Lettuce Wraps

- 3 pounds (1.4 kg) bone-in pork shoulder
- ¾ teaspoon ground cumin
- 1¼ pinches cayenne
- ½ teaspoon black pepper
- ½ teaspoon dried oregano
- ¾ teaspoon garlic powder
- ¾ teaspoon sea salt
- 1¼ tablespoon olive oil
- 1¼ onions, chopped
- 1¼ oranges, juiced
- 2 cups water
- 6 lettuce leaves

1. Put all the ingredients in except the lettuce with the pork and mix them well. Refrigerate overnight.
2. Heat the oil in the instant pot using the Sauté function.

3. Put the marinated pork into the oil and sear for 10 minutes.
4. Pour in 2 cups of water and secure the lid.
5. Select the Manual function and cook for 45 minutes at medium pressure.
6. Release the pressure for 10 minutes using Natural release.
7. Serve the cooked pork on lettuce leaves.

Beef Meatloaf with Mashed Potatoes

Meatloaf:
- 1½ pounds (680 g) ground beef
- 1 onion, diced
- 1 egg
- 1 potato, grated

- ¼ cup tomato purée
- 1 teaspoon garlic powder
- 1 teaspoon salt
- 1 teaspoon ground black pepper

Mashed Potatoes:
- 4 potatoes, chopped
- 2 cups water
- ½ cup milk
- 2 tablespoons olive oil

- 1 teaspoon salt
- ½ teaspoon ground black pepper
- 1 cup ricotta cheese

1. In a bowl, combine ground beef, eggs, 1 teaspoon pepper, garlic powder, potato, onion, tomato purée, and 1 teaspoon salt to obtain a consistent texture. Shape the mixture into a meatloaf and place onto an aluminum foil.
2. Arrange potatoes in the pot and pour water over them. Place a trivet onto the potatoes and set the foil sheet with meatloaf onto trivet. Seal the lid and cook on High Pressure for 22 minutes. Release the pressure quickly.
3. Take the meatloaf from the pot and set on a cutting board to cool before slicing. Drain the liquid out of the pot. Mash potatoes in the pot with ½ teaspoon pepper, milk, ricotta cheese, 1 teaspoon salt, and olive oil until smooth and all the liquid is absorbed.
4. Divide potatoes into serving plates and lean a meatloaf slice to one side of the potato pile before serving.

Beef with Asparagus and Mushroom Sauce

Prep time: 20 minutes | Cook time: 50 minutes | Serves 6

- 3½ pounds (1.6 kg) boneless beef short ribs, cut into pieces
- 2 teaspoons salt
- 1 teaspoon ground black pepper
- 3 tablespoons olive oil
- 1 onion, diced
- 1 cup dry red wine
- 1 tablespoon tomato purée
- 2 carrots, peeled and chopped
- 2 garlic cloves, minced
- 5 sprigs parsley, chopped
- 2 sprigs rosemary, chopped
- 3 sprigs oregano, chopped
- 4 cups beef stock
- 10 ounces (283 g) mushrooms, quartered
- 1 cup asparagus, trimmed chopped
- 1 tablespoon cornstarch
- ¼ cup cold water

1. Season the ribs with black pepper and salt. Warm oil on Sauté. In batches, add the short ribs to the oil and cook for 3 to 5 minutes each side until browned. Set aside. Add onions and sauté for 4 minutes until soft.
2. Add tomato purée and red wine into the pot to deglaze, scrape the bottom to get rid of any browned beef bits. Cook for 2 minutes until wine reduces slightly.
3. Return the ribs to the pot and top with carrots, oregano, rosemary, and garlic. Add broth and press Cancel.
4. Seal the lid, press Meat/Stew and cook on High for 35 minutes. Release pressure naturally for 10 minutes. Transfer ribs to a plate. Strain and get rid of herbs and vegetables, and return cooking broth to inner pot. Add mushrooms and asparagus to the broth. Press Sauté and cook for 2 to 4 minutes until soft.
5. In a bowl, mix water and cornstarch until cornstarch dissolves completely. Add the cornstarch mixture into broth as you stir for 1 to 3 minutes until the broth thickens slightly. Season the sauce with black pepper and salt. Pour the sauce over ribs, add chopped parsley for garnish before serving.

CHAPTER 7

VEGETABLE MAINS

Ratatouille

- 2 large zucchinis, sliced
- 2 medium eggplants, sliced
- 4 medium tomatoes, sliced
- 2 small red onions, sliced
- 4 cloves garlic, chopped
- 2 tablespoons of thyme leaves

- 2 teaspoons sea salt
- 1 teaspoon black pepper
- 2 tablespoons balsamic vinegar
- 4 tablespoons olive oil
- 2 cups water

1. Line a springform pan with foil and place the chopped garlic in the bottom.
2. Now arrange the vegetable slices, alternately, in circles.
3. Sprinkle the thyme, pepper and salt over the vegetables. Top with oil and vinegar.
4. Pour a cup of water into the instant pot and place the trivet inside.
5. Secure the lid and cook on Manual function for 6 minutes at High Pressure.
6. Release the pressure naturally and remove the lid.
7. Remove the vegetables along with the tin foil.
8. Serve on a platter and enjoy.

Mushroom and Potato Teriyaki

- ¾ large yellow or white onion, chopped
- 1½ medium carrots, diced
- 1½ ribs celery, chopped
- 1 medium portabella mushroom, diced
- ¾ tablespoon garlic, chopped
- 2 cups water
- 1 pound (454 g) white potatoes, peeled and diced
- ¼ cup tomato paste
- ½ tablespoon sesame oil
- 2 teaspoons sesame seeds
- ½ tablespoon paprika
- 1 teaspoon fresh rosemary
- ¾ cups peas
- ¼ cup fresh parsley for garnishing, chopped

1. Add the oil, sesame seeds, and all the vegetables in the instant pot and Sauté for 5 minutes.
2. Stir in the remaining ingredients and secure the lid.
3. Cook on Manual function for 13 minutes at High Pressure.
4. After the beep, natural release the pressure and remove the lid.
5. Garnish with fresh parsley and serve hot.

Cauliflower with Sweet Potato

- 1 small onion
- 4 tomatoes
- 4 garlic cloves, chopped
- 2-inch ginger, chopped
- 2 teaspoons olive oil
- 1 teaspoon turmeric
- 2 teaspoons ground cumin
- Salt, to taste
- 1 teaspoon paprika
- 2 medium sweet potatoes, cubed small
- 2 small cauliflowers, diced
- 2 tablespoons fresh cilantro for topping, chopped

1. Blend the tomatoes, garlic, ginger and onion in a blender.
2. Add the oil and cumin in the instant pot and Sauté for 1 minute.
3. Stir in the blended mixture and the remaining spices.
4. Add the sweet potatoes and cook for 5 minutes on Sauté
5. Add the cauliflower chunks and secure the lid.
6. Cook on Manual for 2 minutes at High Pressure.
7. Once done, Quick release the pressure and remove the lid.
8. Stir and serve with cilantro on top.

Potato Curry

- 2 large potatoes, peeled and diced
- 1 small onion, peeled and diced
- 8 ounces (227 g) fresh tomatoes
- 1 tablespoon olive oil
- 1 cup water
- 2 tablespoons garlic cloves, grated
- ½ tablespoon rosemary
- ½ tablespoon cayenne pepper
- 1½ tablespoon thyme
- Salt and pepper to taste

1. Pour a cup of water into the instant pot and place the steamer trivet inside.
2. Place the potatoes and half the garlic over the trivet and sprinkle some salt and pepper on top.
3. Secure the lid and cook on Steam function for 20 minutes.
4. After the beep, natural release the pressure and remove the lid.
5. Put the potatoes to one side and empty the pot.
6. Add the remaining ingredients to the cooker and Sauté for 10 minutes.
7. Use an immerse blender to purée the cooked mixture.
8. Stir in the steamed potatoes and serve hot.

Mushroom Tacos

Prep time: 10 minutes | Cook time: 13 minutes | Serves 3

- 4 large guajillo chilies
- 2 teaspoons oil
- 2 bay leaves
- 2 large onions, sliced
- 2 garlic cloves
- 2 chipotle chillies in adobo sauce
- 2 teaspoons ground cumin
- 1 teaspoon dried oregano
- 1 teaspoon smoked hot paprika
- ½ teaspoon ground cinnamon,
- Salt, to taste
- ¾ cup vegetable broth
- 1 teaspoon apple cider vinegar
- 3 teaspoons lime juice
- ¼ teaspoon sugar
- 8 ounces (227 g) mushrooms chopped
- Whole-wheat tacos, for serving

1. Put the oil, onion, garlic, salt and bay leaves into the instant pot and Sauté for 5 minutes.
2. Blend the half of this mixture, in a blender, with all the spices and chillies.
3. Add the mushrooms to the remaining onions and Sauté for 3 minutes.
4. Pour the blended mixture into the pot and secure the lid.
5. Cook on Manual function for 5 minutes at High Pressure.
6. Once done, Quick release the pressure and remove the lid.
7. Stir well and serve with tacos.

Mushroom and Spinach Stuffed Peppers

Prep time: 15 minutes | Cook time: 8 minutes | Serves 7

- 7 mini sweet peppers
- 1 cup button mushrooms, minced
- 5 ounces (142 g) organic baby spinach
- ½ teaspoon of fresh garlic
- ½ teaspoon of coarse sea salt
- ¼ teaspoon of cracked mixed pepper
- 2 tablespoons water
- 1 tablespoon olive oil
- Organic Mozzarella cheese, diced

1. Put the sweet peppers and water in the instant pot and Sauté for 2 minutes.
2. Remove the peppers and put the olive oil into the pot.
3. Stir in the mushrooms, garlic, spices and spinach.
4. Cook on Sauté until the mixture is dry.
5. Stuff each sweet pepper with the cheese and spinach mixture.
6. Bake the stuffed peppers in an oven for 6 minutes at 400ºF (205ºC).
7. Once done, serve hot.

Cauliflower and Broccoli Bowls

Prep time: 5 minutes | Cook time: 7 minutes | Serves 3

- ½ medium onion, diced
- 2 teaspoons olive oil
- 1 garlic clove, minced
- ½ cup tomato paste
- ½ pound (227 g) frozen cauliflower
- ½ pound (227 g) broccoli florets
- ½ cup vegetable broth
- ½ teaspoon paprika
- ¼ teaspoon dried thyme
- 2 pinches sea salt

1. Add the oil, onion and garlic into the instant pot and Sauté for 2 minutes.
2. Add the broth, tomato paste, cauliflower, broccoli, and all the spices, to the pot.
3. Secure the lid. Cook on the Manual setting at with pressure for 5 minutes.
4. After the beep, Quick release the pressure and remove the lid.
5. Stir well and serve hot.

Black Bean and Corn Tortilla Bowls

Prep time: 10 minutes | Cook time: 8 minutes | Serves 4

- 1½ cups vegetable broth
- ½ cup tomatoes, undrained diced
- 1 small onion, diced
- 2 garlic cloves, finely minced
- 1 teaspoon chili powder
- 1 teaspoon cumin
- ½ teaspoon paprika
- ½ teaspoon ground coriander
- Salt and pepper to taste
- ½ cup carrots, diced
- 2 small potatoes, cubed
- ½ cup bell pepper, chopped
- ½ can black beans, drained and rinsed
- 1 cup frozen corn kernels
- ½ tablespoon lime juice
- 2 tablespoons cilantro for topping, chopped
- Whole-wheat tortilla chips

1. Add the oil and all the vegetables into the instant pot and Sauté for 3 minutes.
2. Add all the spices, corn, lime juice, and broth, along with the beans, to the pot.
3. Seal the lid and cook on Manual setting at High Pressure for 5 minutes.
4. Once done, natural release the pressure when the timer goes off. Remove the lid.
5. To serve, put the prepared mixture into a bowl.
6. Top with tortilla chips and fresh cilantro
7. Serve

Lentils and Eggplant Curry

Prep time: 10 minutes | Cook time: 22 minutes | Serves 4

- ¾ cup lentils, soaked and rinsed
- 1 teaspoon olive oil
- ½ onion, chopped
- 4 garlic cloves, chopped
- 1 teaspoon ginger, chopped
- 1 hot green chili, chopped
- ¼ teaspoon turmeric
- ½ teaspoon ground cumin
- 2 tomatoes, chopped
- 1 cup eggplant, chopped
- 1 cup sweet potatoes, cubed
- ¾ teaspoon salt
- 2 cups water
- 1 cup baby spinach leaves
- Cayenne and lemon/lime to taste
- Pepper flakes (garnish)

1. Add the oil, garlic, ginger, chili and salt into the instant pot and Sauté for 3 minutes.
2. Stir in the tomatoes and all the spices. Cook for 5 minutes.
3. Add all the remaining ingredients, except the spinach leaves and garnish.
4. Secure the lid and cook on Manual function for 12 minutes at High Pressure.
5. After the beep, release the pressure naturally and remove the lid.
6. Stir in the spinach leaves and let the pot simmer for 2 minutes on Sauté.
7. Garnish with the pepper flakes and serve warm.

Sweet Potato and Tomato Curry

Prep time: 5 minutes | Cook time: 8 minutes | Serves 8

- 2 large brown onions, finely diced
- 4 tablespoons olive oil
- 4 teaspoons salt
- 4 large garlic cloves, diced
- 1 red chili, sliced
- 4 tablespoons cilantro, chopped
- 4 teaspoons ground cumin
- 2 teaspoons ground coriander
- 2 teaspoons paprika
- 2 pounds (907 g) sweet potato, diced
- 4 cups chopped, tinned tomatoes
- 2 cups water
- 2 cups vegetable stock
- Lemon juice and cilantro (garnish)

1. Put the oil and onions into the instant pot and Sauté for 5 minutes.
2. Stir in the remaining ingredients and secure the lid.
3. Cook on Manual function for 3 minutes at High Pressure.
4. Once done, Quick release the pressure and remove the lid.
5. Garnish with cilantro and lemon juice.
6. Serve.

Lush Veggie Chili

Prep time: 15 minutes | Cook time: 10 minutes | Serves 3

- ½ tablespoon olive oil
- 1 small yellow onion, chopped
- 4 garlic cloves, minced
- ¾ (15-ounce / 425-g) can diced tomatoes
- 1 ounce (28 g) sugar-free tomato paste
- ½ (4-ounce / 113-g) can green chilies with liquid
- 1 tablespoon Worcestershire sauce
- 2 tablespoons red chili powder
- ½ cup carrots, diced
- ½ cup scallions, chopped
- ½ cup green bell pepper, chopped
- ¼ cup peas
- 1 tablespoon ground cumin
- ½ tablespoon dried oregano, crushed
- Salt and freshly ground black pepper to taste

1. Add the oil, onion, and garlic into the instant pot and Sauté for 5 minutes.
2. Stir in the remaining vegetables and stir-fry for 3 minutes.
3. Add the remaining ingredients and secure the lid.
4. Cook on Manual function for 2 minutes at High Pressure.
5. After the beep, natural release the pressure and remove the lid.
6. Stir well and serve warm.

Carrot and Turnip Purée

Prep time: 10 minutes | Cook time: 10 minutes | Serves 6

- 2 tablespoons olive oil, divided
- 3 large turnips, peeled and quartered
- 4 large carrots, peeled and cut into 2-inch pieces
- 2 cups vegetable broth
- 1 teaspoon salt
- ½ teaspoon ground nutmeg
- 2 tablespoons sour cream

1. Press the Sauté button on Instant Pot. Heat 1 tablespoon olive oil. Toss turnips and carrots in oil for 1 minute. Add broth. Lock lid.
2. Press the Manual button and adjust time to 8 minutes. When timer beeps, quick release pressure until float valve drops and then unlock lid.
3. Drain vegetables and reserve liquid; set liquid aside. Add 2 tablespoons of reserved liquid plus remaining ingredients to vegetables in the Instant Pot. Use an immersion blender to blend until desired smoothness. If too thick, add more liquid 1 tablespoon at a time. Serve warm.

Eggplant and Millet Pilaf

- 1 tablespoon olive oil
- ¼ cup peeled and diced onion
- 1 cup peeled and diced eggplant
- 1 small Roma tomato, seeded and diced
- 1 cup millet
- 2 cups vegetable broth
- 1 teaspoon sea salt
- ¼ teaspoon ground black pepper
- ⅛ teaspoon saffron
- ⅛ teaspoon cayenne pepper
- 1 tablespoon chopped fresh chives

1. Press Sauté button on Instant Pot. Add olive oil. Add onion and cook for 3 to 5 minutes until translucent. Toss in eggplant and stir-fry for 2 more minutes. Add diced tomato.
2. Add millet to Instant Pot in an even layer. Gently pour in broth. Lock lid.
3. Press the Rice button (the Instant Pot will determine the time, about 10 minutes pressurized cooking time). When timer beeps, let pressure release naturally for 5 minutes. Quick release any additional pressure until float valve drops and then unlock lid.
4. Transfer pot ingredients to a serving bowl. Season with salt, pepper, saffron, and cayenne pepper. Garnish with chives.

Potato and Broccoli Medley

- 1 tablespoon olive oil
- ½ white onion, diced
- 1½ cloves garlic, finely chopped
- 1 pound (454 g) potatoes, cut into chunks
- 1 pound (454 g) broccoli florets, diced
- 1 pound (454 g) baby carrots, cut in half
- ¼ cup vegetable broth
- ½ teaspoon Italian seasoning
- ½ teaspoon Spike original seasoning,
- Fresh parsley for garnishing

1. Put the oil and onion into the instant pot and Sauté for 5 minutes.
2. Stir in the carrots, and garlic and stir-fry for 5 minutes.
3. Add the remaining ingredients and secure the lid.
4. Cook on the Manual function for 10 minutes at High Pressure.
5. After the beep, Quick release the pressure and remove the lid.
6. Stir gently and garnish with fresh parsley , then serve.

Radish and Cabbage Congee

Prep time: 5 minutes | Cook time: 20 minutes | Serves 3

- 1 cup carrots, diced
- ½ cup radish, diced
- 6 cups vegetable broth
- Salt, to taste
- 1½ cups short grain rice, rinsed
- 1 tablespoon grated fresh ginger
- 4 cups cabbage, shredded
- Green onions for garnishing, chopped

1. Add all the ingredients, except the cabbage and green onions, into the instant pot.
2. Select the Porridge function and cook on the default time and settings.
3. After the beep, Quick release the pressure and remove the lid
4. Stir in the shredded cabbage and cover with the lid.
5. Serve after 10 minutes with chopped green onions on top.

Mushroom Swoodles

Prep time: 5 minutes | Cook time: 3 minutes | Serves 4

- 2 tablespoons coconut aminos
- 1 tablespoon white vinegar
- 2 teaspoons olive oil
- 1 teaspoon sesame oil
- 1 tablespoon honey
- ¼ teaspoon red pepper flakes
- 3 cloves garlic, minced
- 1 large sweet potato, peeled and spiraled
- 1 pound (454 g) shiitake mushrooms, sliced
- 1 cup vegetable broth
- ¼ cup chopped fresh parsley

1. In a large bowl, whisk together coconut aminos, vinegar, olive oil, sesame oil, honey, red pepper flakes, and garlic.
2. Toss sweet potato and shiitake mushrooms in sauce. Refrigerate covered for 30 minutes.
3. Pour vegetable broth into Instant Pot. Add trivet. Lower steamer basket onto trivet and add the sweet potato mixture to the basket. Lock lid.
4. Press the Manual button and adjust time to 3 minutes. When timer beeps, let pressure release naturally for 5 minutes. Quick release any additional pressure until float valve drops and then unlock lid.
5. Remove basket from the Instant Pot and distribute sweet potatoes and mushrooms evenly among four bowls; pour liquid from the Instant Pot over bowls and garnish with chopped parsley.

Potato, Corn, and Spinach Medley

Prep time: 10 minutes | Cook time: 10 minutes | Serves 6

- 1 tablespoon olive oil
- 3 scallions, chopped
- ½ cup onion, chopped
- 2 large white potatoes, peeled and diced
- 1 tablespoon ginger, grated
- 3 cups frozen corn kernels
- 1 cup vegetable stock
- 1 tablespoon fish sauce
- 2 tablespoons light soy sauce
- 2 large cloves of garlic, diced
- ⅓ teaspoon white pepper
- 1 teaspoon salt
- 3-4 handfuls of baby spinach leaves
- Juice of ½ lemon

1. Put the oil, ginger, garlic and onions in the instant pot and Sauté for 5 minutes.
2. Add all the remaining ingredients except the spinach leaves and lime juice
3. Secure the lid and cook on the Manual setting for 5 minutes at High Pressure.
4. After the beep, Quick release the pressure and remove the lid.
5. Add the spinach and cook for 3 minutes on Sauté
6. Drizzle the lime juice over the dish and serve hot.

Italian Zucchini Pomodoro

Prep time: 10 minutes | Cook time: 12 minutes | Serves 4

- 1 tablespoon avocado oil
- 1 large onion, peeled and diced
- 3 cloves garlic, minced
- 1 (28-ounce / 794-g) can diced tomatoes, including juice
- ½ cup water
- 1 tablespoon Italian seasoning
- 1 teaspoon sea salt
- ½ teaspoon ground black pepper
- 2 medium zucchini, spiraled

1. Press Sauté button on the Instant Pot. Heat avocado oil. Add onions and stir-fry for 3 to 5 minutes until translucent. Add garlic and cook for an additional minute. Add tomatoes, water, Italian seasoning, salt, and pepper. Add zucchini and toss to combine. Lock lid.
2. Press the Manual button and adjust time to 1 minute. When timer beeps, let pressure release naturally for 5 minutes. Quick release any additional pressure until float valve drops and then unlock lid.
3. Transfer zucchini to four bowls. Press Sauté button, press Adjust button to change the temperature to Less, and simmer sauce in the Instant Pot unlidded for 5 minutes. Ladle over zucchini and serve immediately.

Potato and Kale Bowls

Prep time: 10 minutes | Cook time: 10 minutes | Serves 4

- 1 tablespoon olive oil
- 1 small onion, peeled and diced
- 1 stalk celery, diced
- 2 cloves garlic, minced
- 4 medium potatoes, peeled and diced
- 2 bunches kale, washed, deveined, and chopped
- 1½ cups vegetable broth
- 2 teaspoons salt
- ½ teaspoon ground black pepper
- ¼ teaspoon caraway seeds
- 1 tablespoon apple cider vinegar
- 4 tablespoons sour cream

1. Press the Sauté button on Instant Pot. Heat oil. Add onion and celery and stir-fry for 3 to 5 minutes until onions are translucent. Add garlic and cook for an additional minute. Add potatoes in an even layer. Add chopped kale in an even layer. Add broth. Lock lid.
2. Press the Manual button and adjust time to 5 minutes. Let the pressure release naturally for 10 minutes. Quick release any additional pressure until float valve drops and then unlock lid; then drain broth.
3. Stir in salt, pepper, caraway seeds, and vinegar; slightly mash the potatoes in the Instant Pot. Garnish each serving with 1 tablespoon sour cream.

Creamy Potato Curry

Prep time: 10 minutes | Cook time: 18 minutes | Serves 4

- ¾ large yellow or white onion, chopped
- 1½ ribs celery, chopped
- ¼ cup carrots, diced
- ¼ cup green onions
- ½ cup coconut milk
- ¾ tablespoon garlic, chopped
- 1½ cups water
- 1 pound (454 g) white potatoes, peeled and diced
- ¼ cup heavy cream
- ¼ teaspoon thyme
- ¼ teaspoon rosemary
- ½ tablespoon black pepper
- ¾ cup peas
- Salt, to taste
- 2 tablespoons fresh cilantro for garnishing, chopped

1. Add the oil and all the vegetables in the instant pot and Sauté for 5 minutes.
2. Stir in the remaining ingredients and secure the lid.
3. Cook on Manual function for 13 minutes at High Pressure.
4. Once it beeps, natural release the pressure and remove the lid.
5. Garnish with fresh cilantro and serve hot.

Rice, Corn, and Bean Stuffed Peppers

Prep time: 15 minutes | Cook time: 15 minutes | Serves 4

- 4 large bell peppers
- 2 cups cooked white rice
- 1 medium onion, peeled and diced
- 3 small Roma tomatoes, diced
- ¼ cup marinara sauce
- 1 cup corn kernels (cut from the cob is preferred)
- ¼ cup sliced black olives
- ¼ cup canned cannellini beans, rinsed and drained
- ¼ cup canned black beans, rinsed and drained
- 1 teaspoon sea salt
- 1 teaspoon garlic powder
- ½ cup vegetable broth
- 2 tablespoons grated Parmesan cheese

1. Cut off the bell pepper tops as close to the tops as possible. Hollow out and discard seeds. Poke a few small holes in the bottom of the peppers to allow drippings to drain.
2. In a medium bowl, combine remaining ingredients except for broth and Parmesan cheese. Stuff equal amounts of mixture into each of the bell peppers.
3. Place trivet into the Instant Pot and pour in the broth. Set the peppers upright on the trivet. Lock lid.
4. Press the Manual button and adjust time to 15 minutes. When timer beeps, let pressure release naturally until float valve drops and then unlock lid.
5. Serve immediately and garnish with Parmesan cheese.

Cabbage Stuffed Acorn Squash

Prep time: 15 minutes | Cook time: 23 minutes | Serves 4

- ½ tablespoon olive oil
- 2 medium Acorn squashes
- ¼ small yellow onion, chopped
- 1 jalapeño pepper, chopped
- ½ cup green onions, chopped
- ½ cup carrots, chopped
- ¼ cup cabbage, chopped
- 1 garlic clove, minced
- ½ (6-ounce / 170-g) can sugar-free tomato sauce
- ½ tablespoon chili powder
- ½ tablespoon ground cumin
- Salt and freshly ground black pepper to taste
- 2 cups water
- ¼ cup Cheddar cheese, shredded

1. Pour the water into the instant pot and place the trivet inside.
2. Slice the squash into 2 halves and remove the seeds.

3. Place over the trivet, skin side down, and sprinkle some salt and pepper over it.
4. Secure the lid and cook on Manual for 15 minutes at High Pressure.
5. Release the pressure naturally and remove the lid. Empty the pot into a bowl.
6. Now add the oil, onion, and garlic in the instant pot and Sauté for 5 minutes.
7. Stir in the remaining vegetables and stir-fry for 3 minutes.
8. Add the remaining ingredients and secure the lid.
9. Cook on Manual function for 2 minutes at High Pressure.
10. After the beep, natural release the pressure and remove the lid.
11. Stuff the squashes with the prepared mixture and serve warm.

Mushroom and Potato Oat Burgers

Prep time: 20 minutes | Cook time: 21 minutes | Serves 5

- ½ cup minced onion
- 1 teaspoon grated fresh ginger
- ½ cup minced mushrooms
- ½ cup red lentils, rinsed
- ¾ sweet potato, peeled and diced
- 1 cup vegetable stock
- 2 tablespoons hemp seeds
- 2 tablespoons chopped parsley
- 2 tablespoons chopped cilantro
- 1 tablespoon curry powder
- 1 cup quick oats
- Brown rice flour, optional
- 5 tomato slices
- Lettuce leaves
- 5 whole-wheat buns

1. Add the oil, ginger, mushrooms and onion into the instant pot and Sauté for 5 minutes.
2. Stir in the lentils, stock, and the sweet potatoes.
3. Secure the lid and cook on the Manual function for 6 minutes at High Pressure.
4. After the beep, natural release the pressure and remove the lid.
5. Meanwhile, heat the oven to 375ºF (190ºC) and line a baking tray with parchment paper.
6. Mash the prepared lentil mixture with a potato masher.
7. Add the oats and the remaining spices. Put in some brown rice flour if the mixture is not thick enough.
8. Wet your hands and prepare 5 patties, using the mixture, and place them on the baking tray.
9. Bake the patties for 10 minutes in the preheated oven.
10. Slice the buns in half and stack each with a tomato slice, a vegetable patty and lettuce leaves.
11. Serve and enjoy.

Mushroom, Potato, and Green Bean Mix

- 1 tablespoon olive oil
- ½ carrot, peeled and minced
- ½ celery stalk, minced
- ½ small onion, minced
- 1 garlic clove, minced
- ½ teaspoon dried sage, crushed
- ½ teaspoon dried rosemary, crushed
- 4 ounces (113 g) fresh Portabella mushrooms, sliced
- 4 ounces (113 g) fresh white mushrooms, sliced
- ¼ cup red wine
- 1 Yukon Gold potato, peeled and diced
- ¾ cup fresh green beans, trimmed and chopped
- 1 cup tomatoes, chopped
- ½ cup tomato paste
- ½ tablespoon balsamic vinegar
- 3 cups water
- Salt and freshly ground black pepper to taste
- 2 ounces (57 g) frozen peas
- ½ lemon juice
- 2 tablespoons fresh cilantro for garnishing, chopped

1. Put the oil, onion, tomatoes and celery into the instant pot and Sauté for 5 minutes.
2. Stir in the herbs and garlic and cook for 1 minute.
3. Add the mushrooms and sauté for 5 minutes. Stir in the wine and cook for a further 2 minutes
4. Add the diced potatoes and mix. Cover the pot with a lid and let the potatoes cook for 2-3 minutes.
5. Now add the green beans, carrots, tomato paste, peas, salt, pepper, water and vinegar.
6. Secure the lid and cook on Manual function for 8 minutes at High Pressure with the pressure valve in the sealing position.
7. Do a Quick release and open the pot, stir the veggies and then add lemon juice and cilantro, then serve with rice or any other of your choice.

Peanut and Coconut Stuffed Eggplants

- 1 tablespoon coriander seeds
- ½ teaspoon cumin seeds
- ½ teaspoon mustard seeds
- 2 to 3 tablespoons chickpea flour
- 2 tablespoons chopped peanuts
- 2 tablespoons coconut shreds
- 1-inch ginger, chopped
- 2 cloves garlic, chopped
- 1 hot green chili, chopped
- ½ teaspoon ground cardamom
- A pinch of cinnamon
- ⅓ to ½ teaspoon cayenne
- ½ teaspoon turmeric
- ½ teaspoon raw sugar
- ½ to ¾ teaspoon salt
- 1 teaspoon lemon juice
- Water as needed
- 4 baby eggplants
- Fresh Cilantro for garnishing

1. Add the coriander, mustard seeds and cumin in the instant pot.
2. Roast on Sauté function for 2 minutes.
3. Add the chickpea flour, nuts and coconut shred to the pot, and roast for 2 minutes.
4. Blend this mixture in a blender, then transfer to a medium-sized bowl.
5. Roughly blend the ginger, garlic, raw sugar, chili, and all the spices in a blender.
6. Add the water and lemon juice to make a paste. Combine it with the dry flour mixture.
7. Cut the eggplants from one side and stuff with the spice mixture.
8. Add 1 cup of water to the instant pot and place the stuffed eggplants inside.
9. Sprinkle some salt on top and secure the lid.
10. Cook on Manual for 5 minutes at High Pressure, then quick release the steam.
11. Remove the lid and garnish with fresh cilantro, then serve hot.

Appendix 1 Measurement Conversion Chart

VOLUME EQUIVALENTS(DRY)

US STANDARD	METRIC (APPROXIMATE)
1/8 teaspoon	0.5 mL
1/4 teaspoon	1 mL
1/2 teaspoon	2 mL
3/4 teaspoon	4 mL
1 teaspoon	5 mL
1 tablespoon	15 mL
1/4 cup	59 mL
1/2 cup	118 mL
3/4 cup	177 mL
1 cup	235 mL
2 cups	475 mL
3 cups	700 mL
4 cups	1 L

WEIGHT EQUIVALENTS

US STANDARD	METRIC (APPROXIMATE)
1 ounce	28 g
2 ounces	57 g
5 ounces	142 g
10 ounces	284 g
15 ounces	425 g
16 ounces (1 pound)	455 g
1.5 pounds	680 g
2 pounds	907 g

VOLUME EQUIVALENTS(LIQUID)

US STANDARD	US STANDARD (OUNCES)	METRIC (APPROXIMATE)
2 tablespoons	1 fl.oz.	30 mL
1/4 cup	2 fl.oz.	60 mL
1/2 cup	4 fl.oz.	120 mL
1 cup	8 fl.oz.	240 mL
1 1/2 cup	12 fl.oz.	355 mL
2 cups or 1 pint	16 fl.oz.	475 mL
4 cups or 1 quart	32 fl.oz.	1 L
1 gallon	128 fl.oz.	4 L

TEMPERATURES EQUIVALENTS

FAHRENHEIT(F)	CELSIUS(C) (APPROXIMATE)
225 °F	107 °C
250 °F	120 °C
275 °F	135 °C
300 °F	150 °C
325 °F	160 °C
350 °F	180 °C
375 °F	190 °C
400 °F	205 °C
425 °F	220 °C
450 °F	235 °C
475 °F	245 °C
500 °F	260 °C

Appendix 2 Instant Pot Cooking Timetable

Dried Beans, Legumes and Lentils

Dried Beans and Legume	Dry (Minutes)	Soaked (Minutes)
Soy beans	25 – 30	20 – 25
Scarlet runner	20 – 25	10 – 15
Pinto beans	25 – 30	20 – 25
Peas	15 – 20	10 – 15
Navy beans	25 – 30	20 – 25
Lima beans	20 – 25	10 – 15
Lentils, split, yellow (moong dal)	15 – 18	N/A
Lentils, split, red	15 – 18	N/A
Lentils, mini, green (brown)	15 – 20	N/A
Lentils, French green	15 – 20	N/A
Kidney white beans	35 – 40	20 – 25
Kidney red beans	25 – 30	20 – 25
Great Northern beans	25 – 30	20 – 25
Pigeon peas	20 – 25	15 – 20
Chickpeas (garbanzo bean chickpeas)	35 – 40	20 – 25
Cannellini beans	35 – 40	20 – 25
Black-eyed peas	20 – 25	10 – 15
Black beans	20 – 25	10 – 15

Fish and Seafood

Fish and Seafood	Fresh (minutes)	Frozen (minutes)
Shrimp or Prawn	1 to 2	2 to 3
Seafood soup or stock	6 to 7	7 to 9
Mussels	2 to 3	4 to 6
Lobster	3 to 4	4 to 6
Fish, whole (snapper, trout, etc.)	5 to 6	7 to 10
Fish steak	3 to 4	4 to 6
Fish fillet,	2 to 3	3 to 4
Crab	3 to 4	5 to 6

Fruits

Fruits	Fresh (in Minutes)	Dried (in Minutes)
Raisins	N/A	4 to 5
Prunes	2 to 3	4 to 5
Pears, whole	3 to 4	4 to 6
Pears, slices or halves	2 to 3	4 to 5
Peaches	2 to 3	4 to 5
Apricots, whole or halves	2 to 3	3 to 4
Apples, whole	3 to 4	4 to 6
Apples, in slices or pieces	2 to 3	3 to 4

Meat

Meat and Cuts	Cooking Time (minutes)	Meat and Cuts	Cooking Time (minutes)
Veal, roast	35 to 45	Duck, with bones, cut up	10 to 12
Veal, chops	5 to 8	Cornish Hen, whole	10 to 15
Turkey, drumsticks (leg)	15 to 20	Chicken, whole	20 to 25
Turkey, breast, whole, with bones	25 to 30	Chicken, legs, drumsticks, or thighs	10 to 15
Turkey, breast, boneless	15 to 20	Chicken, with bones, cut up	10 to 15
Quail, whole	8 to 10	Chicken, breasts	8 to 10
Pork, ribs	20 to 25	Beef, stew	15 to 20
Pork, loin roast	55 to 60	Beef, shanks	25 to 30
Pork, butt roast	45 to 50	Beef, ribs	25 to 30
Pheasant	20 to 25	Beef, steak, pot roast, round, rump, brisket or blade, small chunks, chuck,	25 to 30
Lamb, stew meat	10 to 15		
Lamb, leg	35 to 45	Beef, pot roast, steak, rump, round, chuck, blade or brisket, large	35 to 40
Lamb, cubes,	10 t0 15		
Ham slice	9 to 12	Beef, ox-tail	40 to 50
Ham picnic shoulder	25 to 30	Beef, meatball	10 to 15
Duck, whole	25 to 30	Beef, dressed	20 to 25

Vegetables (fresh/frozen)

Vegetable	Fresh (minutes)	Frozen (minutes)	Vegetable	Fresh (minutes)	Frozen (minutes)
Zucchini, slices or chunks	2 to 3	3 to 4	Mixed vegetables	2 to 3	3 to 4
Yam, whole, small	10 to 12	12 to 14	Leeks	2 to 4	3 to 5
Yam, whole, large	12 to 15	15 to 19	Greens (collards, beet greens, spinach,	3 to 6	4 to 7
Yam, in cubes	7 to 9	9 to 11	kale, turnip greens, swiss chard) chopped		
Turnip, chunks	2 to 4	4 to 6	Green beans, whole	2 to 3	3 to 4
Tomatoes, whole	3 to 5	5 to 7	Escarole, chopped	1 to 2	2 to 3
Tomatoes, in quarters	2 to 3	4 to 5	Endive	1 to 2	2 to 3
Sweet potato, whole, small	10 to 12	12 to 14	Eggplant, chunks or slices	2 to 3	3 to 4
Sweet potato, whole, large	12 to 15	15 to 19	Corn, on the cob	3 to 4	4 to 5
Sweet potato, in cubes	7 to 9	9 to 11	Corn, kernels	1 to 2	2 to 3
Sweet pepper, slices or chunks	1 to 3	2 to 4	Collard	4 to 5	5 to 6
Squash, butternut, slices or chunks	8 to 10	10 to 12	Celery, chunks	2 to 3	3 to 4
Squash, acorn, slices or chunks	6 to 7	8 to 9	Cauliflower flowerets	2 to 3	3 to 4
Spinach	1 to 2	3 to 4	Carrots, whole or chunked	2 to 3	3 to 4
Rutabaga, slices	3 to 5	4 to 6	Carrots, sliced or shredded	1 to 2	2 to 3
Rutabaga, chunks	4 to 6	6 to 8	Cabbage, red, purple or green, wedges	3 to 4	4 to 5
Pumpkin, small slices or chunks	4 to 5	6 to 7	Cabbage, red, purple or green, shredded	2 to 3	3 to 4
Pumpkin, large slices or chunks	8 to 10	10 to 14	Brussel sprouts, whole	3 to 4	4 to 5
Potatoes, whole, large	12 to 15	15 to 19	Broccoli, stalks	3 to 4	4 to 5
Potatoes, whole, baby	10 to 12	12 to 14	Broccoli, flowerets	2 to 3	3 to 4
Potatoes, in cubes	7 to 9	9 to 11	Beets, small roots, whole	11 to 13	13 to 15
Peas, in the pod	1 to 2	2 to 3	Beets, large roots, whole	20 to 25	25 to 30
Peas, green	1 to 2	2 to 3	Beans, green/yellow or wax,	1 to 2	2 to 3
Parsnips, sliced	1 to 2	2 to 3	whole, trim ends and strings		
Parsnips, chunks	2 to 4	4 to 6	Asparagus, whole or cut	1 to 2	2 to 3
Onions, sliced	2 to 3	3 to 4	Artichoke, whole, trimmed without leaves	9 to 11	11 to 13
Okra	2 to 3	3 to 4	Artichoke, hearts	4 to 5	5 to 6

Rice and Grains

Rice & Grain	Water Quantity (Grain: Water ratios)	Cooking Time (in Minutes)	Rice & Grain	Water Quantity (Grain: Water ratios)	Cooking Time (in Minutes)
Wheat berries	1:3	25 to 30	Oats, steel-cut	1:1	10
Spelt berries	1:3	15 to 20	Oats, quick cooking	1:1	6
Sorghum	1:3	20 to 25	Millet	1:1	10 to 12
Rice, wild	1:3	25 to 30	Kamut, whole	1:3	10 to 12
Rice, white	1:1.5	8	Couscous	1:2	5 to 8
Rice, Jasmine	1:1	4 to 10	Corn, dried, half	1:3	25 to 30
Rice, Brown	1:1.3	22 to 28	Congee, thin	1:6 ~ 1:7	15 to 20
Rice, Basmati	1:1.5	4 to 8	Congee, thick	1:4 ~ 1:5	15 to 20
Quinoa, quick cooking	1:2	8	Barley, pot	1:3 ~ 1:4	25 to 30
Porridge, thin	1:6 ~ 1:7	15 to 20	Barley, pearl	1:4	25 to 30

Appendix 3 The Dirty Dozen and Clean Fifteen

The Environmental Working Group (EWG) is a nonprofit, nonpartisan organization dedicated to protecting human health and the environment Its mission is to empower people to live healthier lives in a healthier environment. This organization publishes an annual list of the twelve kinds of produce, in sequence, that have the highest amount of pesticide residue-the Dirty Dozen-as well as a list of the fifteen kinds ofproduce that have the least amount of pesticide residue-the Clean Fifteen.

THE DIRTY DOZEN

- The 2016 Dirty Dozen includes the following produce. These are considered among the year's most important produce to buy organic:

Strawberries	Spinach
Apples	Tomatoes
Nectarines	Bell peppers
Peaches	Cherry tomatoes
Celery	Cucumbers
Grapes	Kale/collard greens
Cherries	Hot peppers

- *The Dirty Dozen list contains two additional itemskale/collard greens and hot peppers-because they tend to contain trace levels of highly hazardous pesticides.*

THE CLEAN FIFTEEN

- The least critical to buy organically are the Clean Fifteen list. The following are on the 2016 list:

Avocados	Papayas
Corn	Kiw
Pineapples	Eggplant
Cabbage	Honeydew
Sweet peas	Grapefruit
Onions	Cantaloupe
Asparagus	Cauliflower
Mangos	

- *Some of the sweet corn sold in the United States are made from genetically engineered (GE) seedstock. Buy organic varieties of these crops to avoid GE produce.*

Appendix 4 Recipe Index

CPSIA information can be obtained
at www.ICGtesting.com
Printed in the USA
LVHW101647020221
678126LV00001B/56